AUTOCAD 2002

in easy steps

PAUL WHELAN

In easy steps is an imprint of Computer Step
Southfield Road . Southam
Warwickshire CV47 0FB . England

http://www.ineasysteps.com

Notice of Liability

Every effort has been made to ensure that this book contains accurate
and current information. However, Computer Step and the author
shall not be liable for any loss or damage suffered by readers as a
result of any information contained herein.

Trademarks

AutoCAD® is a registered trademark of Autodesk Incorporated. All
other trademarks are acknowledged as belonging to their respective
companies.

Printed and bound in the United Kingdom

ISBN 1-84078-193-9

Contents

Wireframe Construction   155

13

3D Faces   163

14

Rendering   171

15

Working with Paperspace   177

16

Index   189

Fundamental Concepts

In this chapter, you'll learn the difference between traditional draughting techniques and those used in AutoCAD 2002. You will then start AutoCAD 2002 and become familiar with the Create New Drawing dialogue box. Setting the drawing units and the electronic paper size are concepts that must be understood before you draw; these are covered in detail. The layout of the AutoCAD 2002 screen is then described in conjunction with the different methods of giving the program commands.

Covers

Chapter One

Traditional Draughting Techniques

Let us take a look at how you might set about drawing in the traditional way on paper. Before starting to draw, you decide on:

Scale

A scale of 1:1 means one unit on your drawing is the same as one unit in reality.

A drawing of an object that in reality is larger than your sheet of paper (such as an extension to a house), must be scaled down. Something that is too small to represent comfortably on paper (such as the face of a watch), must be scaled up.

Paper size

You must select the sheet of paper the drawing will fit on: e.g. A4, A3, A2, etc.

Units

You're certain to find it useful to know the size of sheets:

The units you use will depend on the conventions expected by the engineers, designers, or builders. You may, for example, work in the imperial or metric systems. Values may be so small that you have to use 'scientific' or exponential notation to dimension a drawing.

A4	=	210*297
A3	=	297*420
A2	=	420*594
A1	=	594*841
A0	=	841*1189

Drawing instruments

Drawing tools such as a T-square, pens, erasers and ruler must be close at hand. Precision drawing tools are expensive and need to be maintained and replaced.

Drawing-board

A good board is essential to aid you in the accurate execution of the drawing.

The drawing process

Much time is spent trying to draw accurately with a pen. AutoCAD 2002 takes care of most of this for you if you learn to use the tools.

During a draughtsperson's traditional training they learn to draw accurately the basic elements of a drawing: lines, arcs, circles, etc. Much time is spent selecting points accurately: the beginning and end points of lines, arcs, etc., and calculating distances.

Construction lines need to be drawn to locate points. Eventually, many of these construction lines will be erased.

AutoCAD Draughting Techniques

AutoCAD 2002 works in Real Size (1=1).

Scale

The problem of scaling is solved in a very dramatic way: there is NO scaling while producing your drawing in AutoCAD 2002. All the dimensions you enter are input in real size (1=1). AutoCAD refers to this as inputting your drawing in Real World Co-ordinates. The computer will of course magnify the image to display it on the screen.

Paper size

When your drawing is completed you decide on the scale you want it printed on paper. A paper size is then selected which can accommodate the drawing.

*If a table is 130cm by 75cm, you draw it 130*75cm in AutoCAD 2002. Similarly, if a watch part has a 0.125mm diameter in reality, it is drawn 0.125 of a millimetre in AutoCAD 2002.*

Electronic paper size

While working in AutoCAD 2002 you draw in real world size (1=1). This means that you must set up an electronic sheet of paper on the computer big enough to hold the drawing at 1=1.

For example, to set up an area on the computer screen to draw a ship of dimensions 210 metres by 32 metres, you must tell AutoCAD that you need an electronic sheet at least 210 by 32 metres. You would probably set up a sheet of 250 by 50 metres. This will be enough space to accommodate the ship.

Units

This command allows you to set up the units you wish to work with.

Drawing instruments

AutoCAD provides 'tools' to help you draw accurately. For example, you can snap onto existing lines or circles.

If you want to draw a building, then the electronic sheet of paper must be a bit bigger than the building!

Drawing board

This instrument has obviously been dispensed with.

The drawing process

AutoCAD 2002 drawings are constructed from pre-defined entities or objects such as lines, arcs and circles. There is a command for each object type (e.g. Line, Arc, Circle, etc.).

Starting and Finishing AutoCAD

Starting AutoCAD 2002 on Windows 95/98/NT/ 2000/Me or XP

Click on the AutoCAD 2002 icon on the desktop. If no icon is present click on 'Start' on the Taskbar. Move the pointer to 'Programs'. Move the pointer to the AutoCAD 2002 folder and click on the AutoCAD 2002 icon.

There is a difference between 'Cancel' and 'OK' on the dialogue boxes: OK keeps the changes you made in the box, whereas Cancel does not.

When AutoCAD 2002 opens it will display the AutoCAD Today dialogue box. This will give you access to the Internet and the drawings on your computer. For the moment just click on the 'Cancel' button. This will display a clean sheet. Read the section below on the dialogue boxes before beginning to work on AutoCAD 2002.

Dialogue boxes

AutoCAD 2002 will display many dialogue boxes while you work. These dialogue boxes will:

• show the current setting the program is working with, and;

• allow you to change some of the settings if you wish.

The 'OK', 'Cancel', 'Close' and 'Done' buttons

If a dialogue box appears which you do not want then click on the 'Cancel' button.

If you do not save your work before you finish the program, it may ask you to 'Save changes to drawing'. The option Cancel will cancel the command to exit from AutoCAD 2002.

If you change any settings in a dialogue box and you want AutoCAD 2002 to use the new settings then click on 'OK'.

'Done' is similar to 'OK'. Click on 'Done' when you have completed modifying a dialogue box.

'Close' will appear on some dialogue boxes. This is similar to 'Cancel'.

You may select the top right button icon 'x' to close the dialogue box without saving any changes.

Finishing AutoCAD 2002

Save your work and then click on the 'x' button or under the File menu: File>Exit.

'Startup' Dialogue Box

The Create Drawings tab will give you access to the Wizard for help in starting the drawing

This dialogue box sets up the electronic sheet size and the units for drawing. To display it, pick the 'Create Drawings' tab in the AutoCad Today dialogue box. Look for 'Select how to begin' and use the down arrow to select 'Wizards' if it is not already selected. Two Wizards are displayed:

• Quick Setup

• Advanced Setup

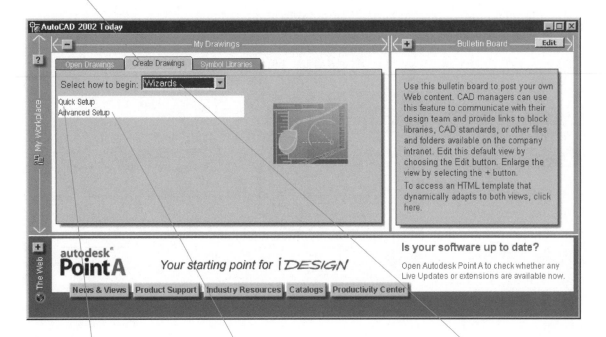

Click here to use the Quick Setup Wizard

The Advanced Setup Wizard will ask you more detailed questions about the settings in your drawing – only use it when you know what you are doing!

This is the Wizard option. It will help you to start a new drawing by asking you some questions

If you do not have the 'Startup' dialogue box on screen, select 'File' from the menu and click on 'New'.

The Drawing Units

The wizard proceeds to the 'Quick Setup' dialogue box. This dialogue box has two options: one for setting up the drawing units and the other to set the size of the electronic page on the computer.

Step 1: Units

AutoCAD 2002 wants to know what units you want to use while drawing. There are five fundamental types of units. Click on each of the units to see a sample.

I unit = I mm

Decimal refers to millimetres (mm).

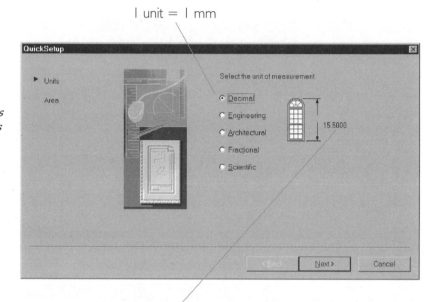

The number of decimal places can be
set later using the Units dialogue box

If you decide not to proceed with the setup, you must click 'Cancel'.

The units selected here will be used by AutoCAD 2002 for dimensioning the drawing. Also, input from the user will be accepted in these units only.

To proceed, select 'Next'.

The Electronic Paper Size

You cannot ignore a dialogue box. It demands a response from you. Clicking on any other part of the computer screen will not banish it. You must click 'Done' or 'Cancel'.

The size of the electronic sheet of paper must be large enough to contain the drawing in real size (1=1). If you are going to plot the finished drawing on standard paper sizes (A3, A2, A1, etc.), then it's a good idea to keep the proportions of the electronic sheet as a multiple of the standard paper sizes.

An example

Imagine the building you must draw is 30 by 20 metres. Convert this to mm by multiplying by 1000 (because you selected decimal (mm) as your unit in 'Step 1'). This is 30*1000 = 30,000mm; 20*1000 = 20,000mm. This building will fit on an A3 sheet (420mm*297mm) multiplied by 100 – i.e. (420mm*297mm)*100 = 42,000*29,700. This is the electronic sheet size you want. It will hold the building in real size (1=1). You can later plot the work onto an A3 sheet by reducing the drawing by a factor of 100 (ie, plot at 1=100).

Step 2: Area

To tell AutoCAD 2002 that this is the electronic sheet size you want, enter 42,000 by 29,700 in the dialogue box (do not type in the thousand separator comma mark).

Double-click here. When the text is highlighted in blue, proceed to type in the electronic page size

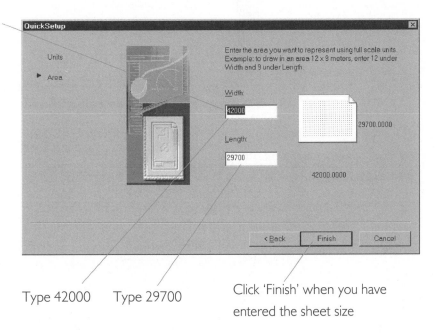

Type 42000   Type 29700   Click 'Finish' when you have entered the sheet size

AutoCAD 2002's Drawing Screen

The current drawing name. If this is 'Drawing?.dwg' it means you have not given the drawing a name yet

The pull-down menus. These contain the drawing and editing commands

The Standard toolbar with frequently used commands

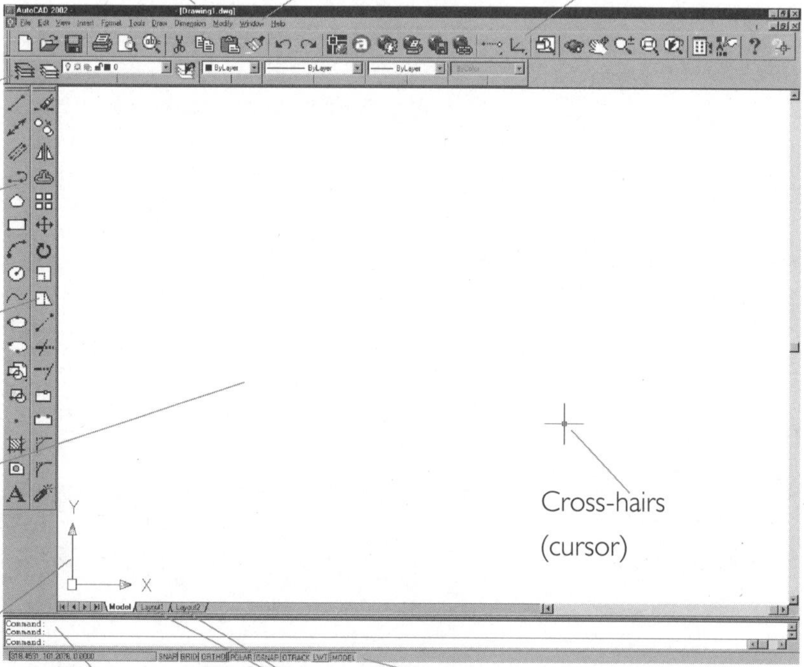

Object Properties toolbar

The 'Draw' toolbar

The 'Modify' toolbar

The drawing editor: this is where you draw

Cross-hairs (cursor)

World co-ordinate system icon: this shows the drawing plane. Its style may be changed

The 'Command line'. You can type commands here and watch for AutoCAD 2002's response

Paperspace or plot layouts

Status bar: shows the available drawing aids and co-ordinates

If the world co-ordinate icon is not visible then switch it on using the command UCSICON and use the option ON.

Saving a Drawing for the First Time,

A drawing which has no name will be titled [Drawing1]. You should give the drawing a name as soon as you set it up. Don't wait until you have drawn some objects. All the settings such as the size of the drawing sheet and the units used are saved as part of the file.

You can call up the 'Save As' dialogue box with the keystrokes *Alt+F and then A. That is, hold down the Alt key and press F. This will drop-down the menu. Then press A, the underlined letter in 'Save As'.*

Save and Save As

There are two ways to save the drawing. Both ways are found on the File drop-down menu. One is to use the 'Save' command and the other method is the 'Save As' command. Generally, 'Save As' is used if (1) you are saving a drawing for the first time (as in this case), and (2) if the drawing already has a name (other than 'Drawing') and you want to rename it as something else. Use 'Save' if the drawing already has a name.

1 Click on the drop-down menu 'File'.

2 Click on 'Save As'. The 'Save Drawing As' dialogue appears.

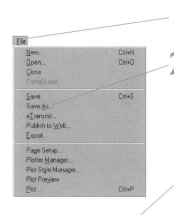

The drawing will be saved into the folder that is open here

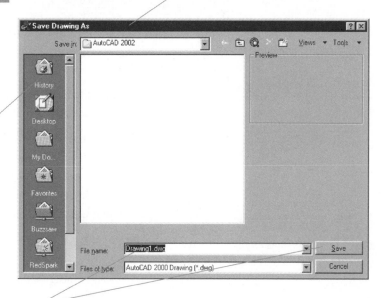

3 Type in a file name and click on 'Save'. AutoCAD 2002 can take long, descriptive file names.

Giving AutoCAD 2002 Commands

Pull-down menus

Just click on the menu name to see the list of commands. Click on a command to issue it. If a command has an arrow after it, a sub-menu will appear when you move the arrow cursor over it. Click on a command in the sub-menu to issue it. If a pull-down menu item is followed by three omission points then a dialogue box will appear when it is selected.

If you use a short-cut you do not need to pull down a menu. Ctrl+S will save the drawing.

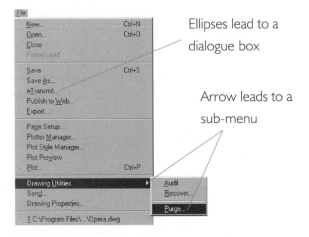

Ellipses lead to a dialogue box

Arrow leads to a sub-menu

Using Alt+

The pull-down menus may also be selected by using 'Alt+ the underlined letter from the menu'. For example, hold down the Alt key and press the 'F' key to pull down the 'File' menu.

Right-clicking

If you position the mouse pointer over the menus or toolbars and right-click, a floating menu will appear displaying a list of the available toolbars.

Try right-clicking over the Drawing Editor and then over the Standard toolbar to see the context-sensitive menus in action.

Shortcuts

For example, Ctrl+S will issue the save command even if the pull down menu is not activated.

...cont'd

Toolbars can be dragged out on to the drawing editor where they become floating toolbars. These floating toolbars can be moved around the screen.

You must keep your eye on the command line when drawing and editing. AutoCAD 2002 'talks' to you there.

Toolbars

Many commands can be issued by just picking the appropriate icon from the toolbars.

Cursor menu

These menus are called up by using the shift key and a mouse button other than the 'click' (or left mouse) button:

If you have a two button mouse hold shift down and right-click.

If you have a three button mouse or an IntelliMouse use shift and the middle button or the wheel.

The command line

The command line at the bottom of the drawing editor is very important in drawing with AutoCAD 2002. You must keep checking what is written at this line as you draw and edit.

For example, if you draw a line AutoCAD 2002 will need to know where the line starts and ends. It will ask for these locations at the command line.

Again, if you want to erase a line or a circle, AutoCAD 2002 will ask you which line or circle at the command line. The importance of the command line cannot be over emphasised.

Here are two examples of the command line requesting input from the user:

AutoCAD 2002 wants to know where the line is to start

L for line

```
|◄ ◄ ► ►| \ Model ╱ Layout1 ╱ Layout2 ╱
Command: L
LINE Specify first point:
129.3048, 273.8469, 0.0000        SNAP GRID ORTHO POLAR OSNAP OTRACK LWT MODEL
```

AutoCAD 2002 is requesting the location of the centre point of the circle

C for circle

```
|◄ ◄ ► ►| \ Model ╱ Layout1 ╱ Layout2 ╱
Command: C
CIRCLE Specify center point for circle or [3P/2P/Ttr (tan tan radius)]:
308.3904, 225.0239, 0.0000        SNAP GRID ORTHO POLAR OSNAP OTRACK LWT MODEL
```

Opening an Existing Drawing

To open an already existing drawing, click on File>Open, or click the 'Open Folder' icon. This will display the Select File dialogue box. Make sure you are looking in the correct folder. The list of drawings in this dialogue box will have the letters 'dwg' at the end of each file name, which indicates that they are drawing files.

Select the file you want to open by first highlighting it. A preview (or miniature image) of the selected drawing will appear in the Preview screen. Click on Open to load the selected file into AutoCAD 2002:

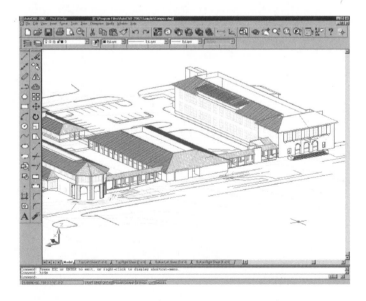

Basic Drawing Techniques

In this chapter, you'll learn the basic drawing techniques employed by AutoCAD 2002. Great emphasis is placed on reading what is displayed at the command line. Recovering from errors in both your use of AutoCAD 2002 and in creating a drawing is outlined. The commands for drawing a circle and moving an entity are examined in detail. Mastering these commands is essential if you want to make progress in understanding what AutoCAD 2002 expects from you, the user.

As a further aid to drawing accurately, we will look at the idea of snapping to an object using the end point of a line and the centre of a circle as examples. Finally, you will learn how to switch these Object Snap options on as background tools.

Covers

Chapter Two

Drawing a Line

Use the short-cut Ctrl+S to save the drawing regularly.

The command **LINE** (or simply **L** typed at the command line) will draw line entities in the drawing editor.

How the command works

When the command is executed, AutoCAD 2002 will ask you to specify the starting and end points of the line. Remember, you can use the command line, the drop-down menu or the toolbar. *Regardless of the method you use to give the command, you must look down at the command line to see how AutoCAD 2002 is responding.*

Instead of pressing Enter you could just press the Spacebar, or press the right mouse button and select Enter from the floating menu.

Use one of these methods:

*   At the command line just type L and press Enter

*   On the drop-down menu 'Draw,' click on Line

*   On the toolbar click on the line icon

AutoCAD 2002 will ask 'Specify the first point:'. Click on a point and move the mouse. AutoCAD 2002 will now ask 'Specify the next point or [Undo]:'. Respond by clicking another point. AutoCAD 2002 will keep asking 'Specify the next point or [Close/Undo]:' until you finish the command by pressing Enter.

The Line icon

Click on the first point in response to 'Specify the first point:'

AutoCAD 2002 will keep asking 'Specify next point or [Undo]:' until you press Enter to terminate the command

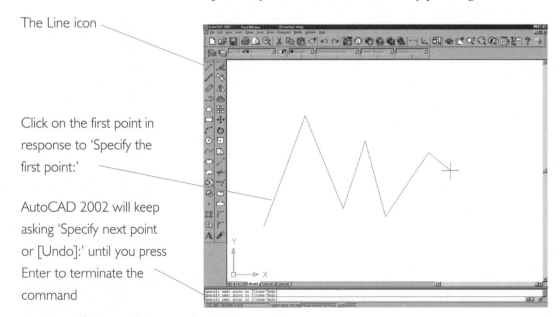

What to Do If You Make a Mistake

Two types of mistakes frequently occur: mistakes associated with using AutoCAD 2002 itself and mistakes in the actual drawing you are working on.

Pressing the ESC key

The Esc key at the top left of the keyboard will get you out of most problems you encounter in using AutoCAD 2002. Here are some examples of the times you would press the Esc key:

- If a command is not responding the way you expect

- If you want to cancel a command you started

- If you clicked a point on the screen unintentionally

- If a dialogue box appears on the screen accidentally

In all the cases above, pressing Esc once will free up the command line. When the command line is blank you can proceed to issue a new command. In some cases you may need to press the Esc key two or even three times. For example, if you are dimensioning an entity and you decide you would like to return to a blank command line or if little blue boxes called grips appear on objects.

Example

Issue the Line command, click a point on the screen and then press the Esc key to cancel the command.

Without issuing a command just pick a point in the drawing editor. A window will appear as you move the mouse. Press Esc to cancel out of it.

Using Undo

You can undo the last command by typing U at the command line and pressing the Enter key, or by clicking on the Undo icon on the toolbar.

Using Redo

The Redo command will reinstate the last command you applied undo to. You may undo as many commands as you like, but you may only redo once. Redo must follow the Undo command. The Redo icon is beside Undo.

Drawing a Circle

If you do not keep your eye on the command line you will not be able to use AutoCAD 2002.

To draw a circle, use the following:

Command line: circle, or the alias 'c'

Menu: Draw>Circle

Toolbar:

How the command works

The <angled brackets> show the option that AutoCAD 2002 is offering you.

When the Circle command is issued AutoCAD 2002 will need to know where the centre of the circle is to be and its radius or diameter. The command line will prompt 'Circle Specify center point for circle or [3P/2P/Ttr (tan tan radius)]:'. Pick a point on the screen as the centre of the circle. If you don't want to click the centre of the circle and instead use a different option, you must type the capitalised letter(s) of the option required. To draw a circle through three specified points you enter 3P at the command line and press the enter key. T must be typed to draw a circle with a radius that is a tangent to two objects.

Drawing with the Circle default options

To select an option other than the default, you must type in the capitalised letter(s) offered at the command prompt.

In response to 'Circle Specify center point for circle or [3P/2P/Ttr (tan tan radius)]:' click a point on the screen. The command line displays 'Specify radius of circle or [Diameter] <xxx>:'. Radius is the default option. If you move the mouse a circle will form, determined by the size of the radius you are showing AutoCAD 2002. Click on a point. AutoCAD 2002 draws a circle and the command line is left blank.

The 'circle' command ends on its own, whereas the line command continues until you press Enter or the Spacebar to terminate it.

Various options for drawing a circle are shown on this menu

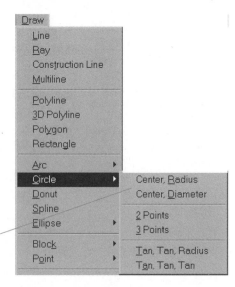

Moving an Object

To tell AutoCAD 2002 you have finished selecting objects, just press the Enter key.

To move any entity:

Command line: move, or the alias 'm'

Menu: Modify>Move

Toolbar:

How the command works

AutoCAD 2002 will need to know what object you want to move. This requires that you select the object or objects. You will then need to specify where you want to pick up the object and lastly where you will place it. If you wish you can give the distance you want to displace or move the object.

If you miss the object you are trying to select, a box will appear at the cursor. Just move the box so it crosses over the entity and click again.

Using the Move command

Issue the Move command. The command line displays 'Select objects:' and the cursor will change to a pickbox. Place the pickbox over the circle's perimeter and click once. The circle will be highlighted if you succeed. The prompt shows 'Select objects: 1 found', Select objects:'. At this point you press Enter or the right button on the mouse to tell AutoCAD 2002 that you have finished selecting objects. The command line changes to 'Specify base point or displacement:'. AutoCAD 2002 wants to know where you will pick up the object. Click anywhere near or on the circle. The command line displays 'Specify second point of displacement'. Now you can move the circle by moving the mouse and pick the location you want to position the circle. The command will terminate itself and give you a blank command line.

If the pickbox is too small, just type 'pickbox' at the command line and increase its value. The default size is 3.

You can use polar co-ordinates to move an object an exact distance.

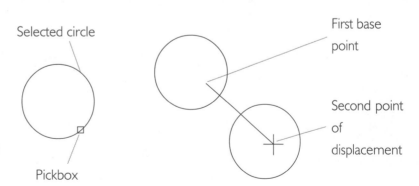

Selected circle

Pickbox

First base point

Second point of displacement

Using Grid and Snap

The F7 key toggles the grid on/off or use the status line.

The Grid

The grid is an array of dots placed over the drawing. It is a drawing aid and will not print – it is not part of the drawing. A grid has three main functions: it shows you the size of the electronic sheet you set up; you can snap the cross-hairs to the grid; when you magnify the drawing with the zoom command the distance between the grid points will give you an idea of how much you have magnified the image. The grid can be switched on/off at any time using the status line by single-clicking on it.

The size of the grid may be changed at any time by typing GRID at the command line and entering a new value.

Snap

When snap is not active, the cross-hairs move smoothly across the drawing editor. Snap causes the cross-hairs to move in jumps. For example, setting the snap to 25mm will allow you to quickly draw lines of 25mm or multiples thereof. You will not be able to draw between the 25mm setting unless you switch snap off. Often the snap and grid setting are the same (say 25mm) but they do not have to be equal. Snap can be switched on/off from the status line.

Snap is useful for doing a quick sketch with straight edges.

The F9 key toggles the snap on/off or use the status line.

You can also use a special snap to lock on to the objects you have already drawn. See Object Snap on page 26.

Ortho

Ortho mode allows you to draw lines either vertically or horizontally. The F8 key toggles the ortho mode on and off. You can also single-click on ORTHO on the status line.

If you draw outside the grid area, you are drawing outside the electronic page you set up.

The Ortho mode is the equivalent of using a T square in traditional draughting.

If the grid setting is too small, AutoCAD 2002 will refuse to display it.

| SNAP | GRID | ORTHO | POLAR | OSNAP | OTRACK | LWT | MODEL |

Switches Snap, Grid and Ortho modes on/off with a single-click

Drafting Settings – Snap and Grid

Right click on the Grid or Snap buttons on the Status line and select

Settings:

AutoCAD 2002 has several drafting aids. These are accessed through the menu Tools>Drafting Settings. The dialogue box below is displayed. It has three tabs: make the Snap & Grid tab current by clicking on it. It's a good idea to look at this dialogue box before you start working. All the settings can be changed at any time during the drawing procedure.

The most important aids are the Grid, Snap and Ortho features. The Isometric Snap is only for isometric drawing. It sets up three isoplanes. In this mode a circle will appear elliptical.

Switches the Grid on/off

Sets the size of the grid in the current drawing units

Switches the Snap on/off

Sets the snap distance horizontally

Sets the snap distance vertically

Sets the angle that the snap runs at

Sets the snap origin – useful to align the snap with an object

Sets the snap to the grid value

Sets the snap and grid for Standard or non-Isometric mode.

Sets the snap and grid for Isometric mode.

Sets the snap to follow the polar angle setting instead of the grid

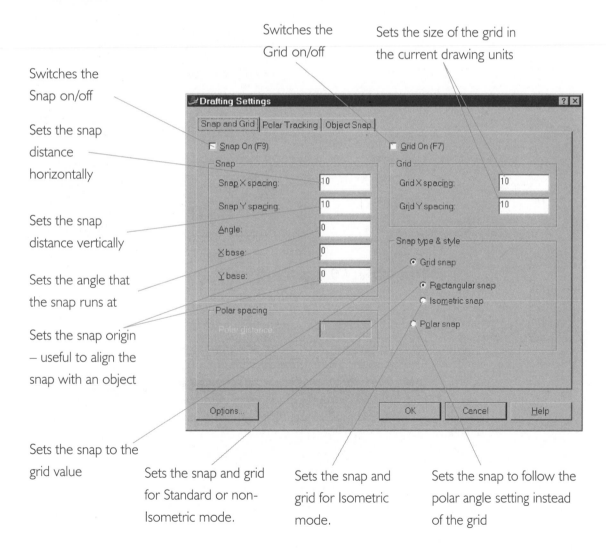

Snapping to Objects – the Toolbar

A toolbar can be dragged to any location on the screen and resized.

By their nature CAD drawings have to be accurate. Joining drawing objects such as lines, arcs and circles should never be done just using your eye. AutoCAD 2002 has many tools to allow you to lock on to the end of a line or the centre of a circle. These are known as the Object Snap tools and are found on the Object Snap toolbar.

To display the Object Snap toolbar

Choose View>Toolbars...

The following displays (ensure the Toolbars tab is active):

List of available toolbars

The Toolbars dialogue box can be called up by moving the cursor over any existing toolbar and right-clicking and selecting Customise.

Tick displays the toolbar

Click once to place/remove the tick

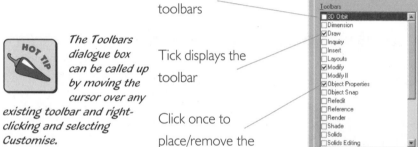

The Object Snap Toolbar

Do not use snap and Object Snap at the same time.

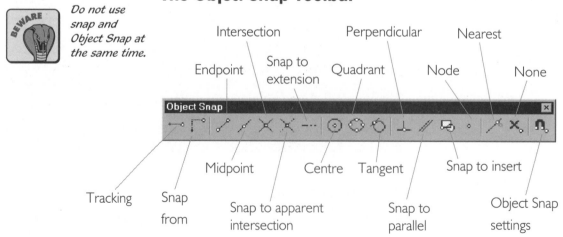

Snapping to Objects – an Example

Display the Object Snap toolbar (see page 26). Draw a line and a circle near each other on the screen. Now move the circle using Object Snap to the end of the line so that the centre of the circle is located exactly on the end of the line, as follows:

If you fail to read what is displayed at the command line, you will not be able to draw with accuracy.

1   Issue the Move command and read the command line.

2   Pick the circle in response to 'select objects'.

3   Press Enter or the right button on the mouse to tell AutoCAD 2002 that there is nothing else you want to select.

4   In response to 'Specify base point or displacement' click on 'Snap to Center' from the Object Snap toolbar. The command line now displays 'cen of' (meaning centre of).

Always use the Object Snap to ensure accuracy.

5   Move the mouse down to the periphery of the selected circle. When a small coloured (usually yellow or red) selection circle appears at the centre of the selected circle, click the left mouse button.

6   AutoCAD 2002 will pick up the circle at its centre point and the command line will display 'Specify second point of displacement:'

7   Click on 'Snap to Endpoint' from the Object Snap toolbar and move the cursor down over the line towards the end you want to place the circle. The command line will display 'endp of'.

Never try to join objects by relying on your eye. Always snap to objects.

8   A coloured selection box will appear towards one end of the line. Click when you see this. The circle will lock into position.

Running Object Snap Tools

If you find the cursor behaving in a way you do not understand, try switching off the Object Snap. It's easy to forget you have it on.

Where you are doing a lot of editing, you may find that you are constantly selecting from the Object Snap toolbar. You can overcome this by setting up a running Object Snap. This allows you to preset and switch on the Object Snaps you frequently use. When the running Object Snap is switched on, the cursor will automatically select those snaps as soon as you approach an entity.

Setting up the Object Snap

Command line: osnap, or the alias 'os'

Menu: Tools>Drafting Settings

Status Bar: Right click on OSNAP.

Once the running Object Snap is set up, it can be toggled on/off by single-clicking OSNAP on the status line.

The following menu will appear:

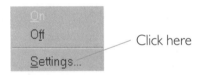

Click here

The following dialogue box will appear:

Place a tick in the Object Snaps you want to use

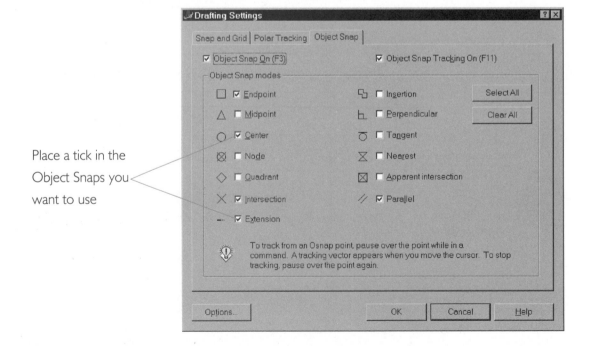

Accuracy and Speed

In this chapter, you'll learn how to speed up drawing and editing by using some of AutoCAD 2002's sophisticated tools. Aliases, aerial views and snapping to objects will increase speed and accuracy dramatically. It is worth concentrating on these until they are mastered. Using co-ordinate input is essential for any work that requires specific dimensions. You may think you can survive without grips – until you know how to use them! They save time and ensure accuracy.

Covers

Chapter Three

Opening an Existing Drawing

AutoCAD 2002 allows you to open several drawings at once. Each drawing is contained within its own document window.

Double-clicking on a file name will open it automatically into AutoCAD 2002.

Command line: open

Menu: File>Open

Toolbar: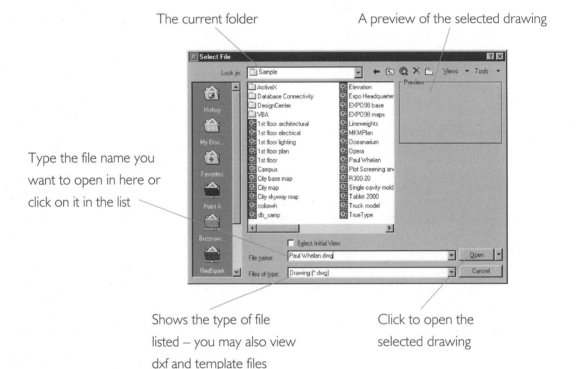

The Select File dialogue box will then open.

The current folder   A preview of the selected drawing

Type the file name you want to open in here or click on it in the list

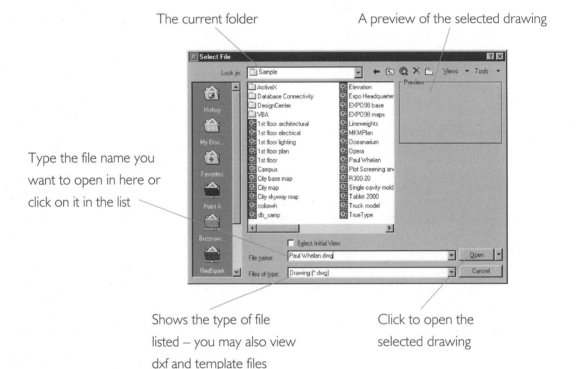

Shows the type of file listed – you may also view dxf and template files

Click to open the selected drawing

By keeping the Ctrl key depressed while selecting drawings, you can select several drawings at once.

Multiple Design Environment

Not only will AutoCAD 2002 allow you to open several drawings at the same time, but you can also take the properties of objects such as colour, layers, linetype scales and linetypes, from one drawing to another using Windows Explorer. Also a command can be left running in one drawing while you move back to another. These features allow you speed up the drawing and design process.

Using Co-ordinate Input

You cannot type a space when inputting the co-ordinates.

AutoCAD 2002 has several ways to input co-ordinates to specify the length of objects, or their angle of orientation. Co-ordinate input can also be used to specify the distance over which objects can be copied, moved or stretched. Gaps can be made in objects – e.g. by inputting the width of the gap in polar co-ordinates. Absolute, relative and polar co-ordinates will be described below.

Absolute co-ordinates

This co-ordinate system relies on the location of the origin 0,0. The origin is normally located at the bottom left of the screen. The X and Y axis meet at the origin. An absolute co-ordinate is input as two numbers separated by a comma. The first number is the distance along the X axis and the second number the distance on the Y axis.

For example, to draw a line from the origin:

The @ symbol means 'from the last point'.

Command: L	(Type L and press Enter)
LINE Specify first point: 0,0	(Type in 0,0 and Enter)
Specify next point: or [Undo]:100,100	(Type in 100,100 and Enter)
Specify next point or [Close/Undo]:	(Press Enter)

Relative co-ordinates

This co-ordinate system relies on the location of the last point entered. The @ symbol is entered before the co-ordinate. It means from the last position. A co-ordinate @45,67 specifies a location 45 units along the X axis and 67 units along the Y axis *relative* to the last location.

Polar co-ordinates

This co-ordinate system allows you to specify a distance and angle from the last point. It takes the format:

You can only use the @ symbol whilst in an AutoCAD 2002 command.

From the last point   Give as drawing units   Symbol for angle

@distance<n

Angle value between 0 and 360

e.g.:   @322<90

Co-ordinate Input – Examples

You do not have to pick the first point of displacement on the object you are moving.

Polar co-ordinates can be used any time that AutoCAD 2002 asks for a displacement or a new point. To follow these examples, set a page size of 420 by 297 in decimal units.

Drawing a line – absolute and polar co-ordinates

Issue the Line command. Read the command line and enter an absolute co-ordinate of 0,0 and press Enter. A line will run from the origin out to the cross hairs. In response to 'Specify next point' type in the polar co-ordinate @50<45. A line 50 mm long at an angle of 45 degrees will be drawn. Continue with the following values in response to 'Specify next point': @100<0, @200<90, @100<180, @100<270. Press the right mouse button and select Enter to finish the command.

If you accidentally terminate the current command, then use Object Snap to pick up from the end of the last line endpoint and just proceed with the polar co-ordinates.

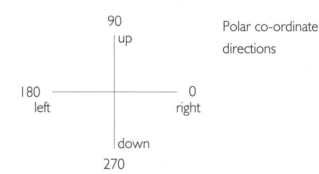

Moving a line by polar co-ordinates

Let us imagine you have to move the right vertical line 25mm to the right (0 degrees direction). Issue the Move command. Click on the right vertical line when asked to 'Select objects'. Right click to tell AutoCAD 2002 that you have finished selecting objects. In response to 'Specify base point or displacement' click anywhere on the screen (click near the line). In response to 'Specify second point of displacement' type in @25<0 and press Enter. The line will be moved 25mm to the right.

Direction is input at an angle in polar co-ordinates.

Try doing this with the Copy command.

Using the Zoom Toolbar

Zoom allows you to change the magnification of your drawing view. The Zoom toolbar may be accessed from the Standard Toolbar at the top of the screen or from the drop down menu View>Toolbars...>Zoom. The icons are:

If you get lost press the Esc key and try again.

Zoom window icon: this allows you to select a window or box around the area you want to magnify

Zoom dynamic: this is both a zoom and a pan. When the command is issued a view box will be displayed with the drawing inside. The view box can be resized (zoom) and moved around (pan)

Zoom scale: the drawing is at a scale of 1. A zoom scale of 2 doubles the magnification of the drawing, while 0.5 halves it

Zoom center: allows you to pick a point which will be the center of the zoom area.

Zoom in: just click on it to zoom in on the drawing. You may preset the amount it zooms in at the command line

Zoom out: just click on it to zoom out from the drawing. You may preset the amount it zooms out at the command line

You can pan and zoom using the command line. Type zoom or z and pan or p and press Enter.

Zoom all: this zooms to show the complete electronic page you set up. It zooms out to the electronic sheet limits

Zoom extents: this will zoom to fit the complete drawing on the screen

Aerial View

Aerial view is exceptionally useful if you are working on a drawing that occupies a large area. It enables you to view the whole drawing in a small window within the drawing editor. Panning and zooming in the smaller aerial view window will be reflected in the editor. The aerial view window can be dragged around the screen, minimised, maximised and closed as usual for all windows.

The aerial view can be called up by typing 'dsviewer' at the command line.

Aerial view is most useful for large complex drawings.

Aerial view window

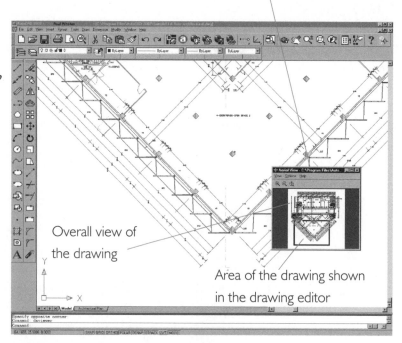

Overall view of the drawing

Area of the drawing shown in the drawing editor

You cannot draw or edit inside the aerial view window.

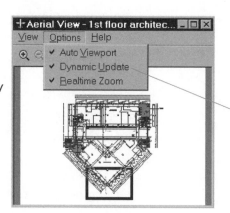

Aerial view can immediately show changes made to the drawing in the drawing editor if Dynamic Update is ticked under its Options menu

The Purge Command

To purge a drawing is to remove any references in the drawing to unused linetypes, text styles, layers, blocks, etc. A drawing which has been purged is often smaller in size and much more stable than an unpurged drawing. It is good practice to purge a drawing before you store it permanently or give it to another person. Always purge a drawing before you send it via email, for example.

A drawing which has never been purged can become unstable.

While constructing a drawing you may make a layer or load a linetype and find that you never use it. Purge will remove any reference to them.

To issue the command

Type 'purge' at the command line and press Enter. The prompt 'All items' will allow you to purge blocks, layers, etc. The other options allow you to select objects individually.

The drop-down option is under the File menu 'Drawing Utilities'.

Purge needs to be run several times as it only works to one level of reference at a time. Keep purging until you see the message 'No unreferenced x to purge'

Purge will not delete anything which is used in the drawing.

How to Select Objects

Objects in the drawing editor need to be selected regularly while drawing and editing. Using the pickbox to select individual elements is a commonly used technique. However there are several other ways which are particularly useful for selecting several objects. Some of these methods are described here.

Imagine that the command line displays 'Select objects:' The following selection methods work:

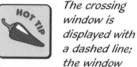

The crossing window is displayed with a dashed line; the window method shows a window displayed by a continuous line.

1 All: this selects all objects in the drawing except those on layers that are thawed (for more on this, see Chapter Seven, *Working with Layers* in this book's companion title, 'AutoCAD LT in easy steps'). This is useful if you wish to move the whole drawing to a new location on the page.

2 l: l is for last. The last object you worked on will be selected.

3 p: p is for previous. The last objects you selected will be selected.

4 f: f is for fence. You can select points on the screen through which AutoCAD 2002 draws a fence line. Objects which the fence cross are selected.

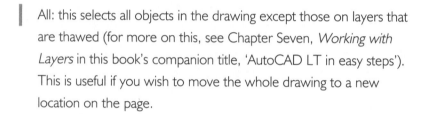

Cursor

Crossed lines are selected

Fence

Claret

Don't limit yourself to the same selection options all the time. Being familiar with several will add speed and accuracy to your work.

5 cp: cp means crossing polygon. This time the 'fence' is called a polygon. Construct it the same way as the fence. Objects selected either cross the polygon or are completely inside it.

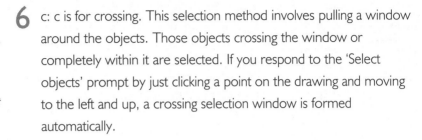

...cont'd

Don't bother pressing 'c' for a crossing window, just click and move the cursor from right to left for a crossing box.

6 c: c is for crossing. This selection method involves pulling a window around the objects. Those objects crossing the window or completely within it are selected. If you respond to the 'Select objects' prompt by just clicking a point on the drawing and moving to the left and up, a crossing selection window is formed automatically.

7 w: w is for window. Pull a window around the object(s). Those objects completely within the window will be highlighted. If you don't respond to the 'select objects' prompt with 'w', just drag a window from right to left. This will automatically form a selection window.

An object can be deselected by holding down the Shift key and clicking on it while AutoCAD is asking 'Select objects'.

8 wp: this is a polygon window. Objects must be completely within the polygon for selection.

9 r: r is for remove. This invaluable option allows you to deselect objects which you accidentally selected.

The crossing window is a dashed box

All the objects crossing the window will be selected along with those completely inside the window

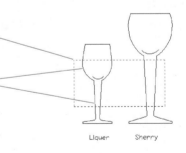

Liquer   Sherry

You can mix the selection methods. For example, start with a crossing window and continue with a fence or a single click selection.

The complete selection window is a continuous box

Only this arc will be selected

Grips – the Little Blue Boxes

Grips can be applied to several entities at once by dragging a window around them.

You have probably experienced little blue boxes appearing on objects in the drawing editor. They are called Grips. Pressing the Esc key twice will remove them. Grips appear if you select an object while the command line is blank. They appear at specific points on an object such as the endpoints and midpoint of a line. Grips can be dragged to perform actions such as rotating, moving or scaling the object.

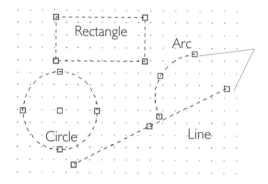

Grips on objects – each square is a grip

Right-clicking when a grip is highlighted will bring up the commands associated with it.

To call up the grips dialogue box use Tools>Options and pick the Selection tab, or at the command line type ddgrips. The grips can also be switched on/off by entering 1 for 'on' and 0 for 'off' in response to the typed command grips.

A tick here allows the grips to function

Sets the colour for selected and unselected grips

Sets the size of the grip box

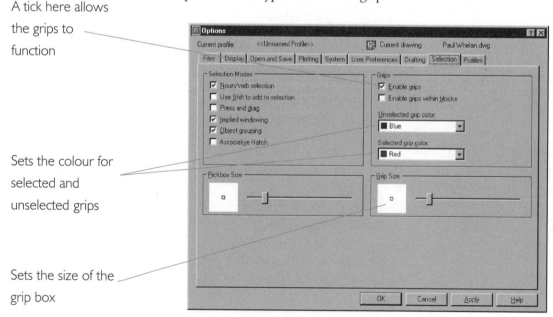

How to Use the Grips

Grips allow you to apply the following commands to an object: Stretch, Move, Rotate, Scale and Mirror.

To try out these options, draw a separate line and circle.

Default options are always shown inside angle brackets <>.

Moving a circle with grips

Without issuing a command, click on the circle. Grips will appear. Now click on the centre-point grip. It will become a solid colour (red is the default). The command line shows:

STRETCH

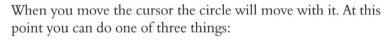
<Specify stretch point or [Base point/Copy/Undo/eXit]:

To see the other commands press the Spacebar or the Enter key. Keep pressing it until you see the Move command. The command line will then show:

Specify move point or [Base point/Copy/Undo/eXit]:

Cycle through the Grip options by pressing either the Spacebar or the Enter key.

When you move the cursor the circle will move with it. At this point you can do one of three things:

- just click a point on the screen to reposition the circle
- use polar co-ordinates to re-locate it accurately
- use Object Snap to snap to another object

To remove the grips press the Esc key twice.

Stretching a line with grips

Select the line. The grips will appear. Click on one of the endpoints to highlight a grip. Press the Spacebar or the Enter key until you find:

STRETCH

Use polar co-ordinates or Object Snap in conjunction with grips for greater accuracy.

<Specify stretch point or [Base point/Copy/Undo/eXit]:

At this point you can do one of three things:

- just click a point on the screen to stretch the line
- use polar co-ordinates to stretch it a specific distance
- use Object Snap to snap to another object

System Variables

System variables hold specific settings or values that affect how the AutoCAD 2002 system works. By changing a variable you specify how a command might function or how the AutoCAD 2002 screen looks. Some useful system variables are described here.

Blipmode

This controls the display of small '+' symbols called blips, at selection points on the screen. It is set to 'off' in AutoCAD 2002. Try switching it on and draw a line to see the effect. At the command line type 'Blipmode' and press the Spacebar or Enter. Type 'On' or 'Off'. The default setting is shown in angled brackets. Blips are not part of the drawing. They will not be printed. The Redraw command (or just R and Enter) will remove the blips on the display.

If AutoCAD 2002 is not working the way that you have come to expect, then check the system variables. Someone might have changed some.

Mirrtext

This variable controls how text is mirrored when you use the Mirror command. If text is mirrored when the variable is set to 1 (the default value), the text will appear inverted (exactly as it would appear in a real mirror). If the Mirrtext variable is set to 0, the text will appear normal (legible). Type 'Mirrtext' at the command line to change it.

Ucsicon

The image of the X and Y axis at the bottom left of the screen is controlled by this system variable. It can be switched on or off by typing 'Ucsicon' at the command line.

Filedia

Controls the display of the dialogue boxes associated with file commands such as the Save and Save As. There are two settings – 1 causes the boxes to be displayed (this is the default); 0 prevents their display. If a dialogue box is not displayed you must read the command line to save the files. Type 'Filedia' to change the settings.

Users of the pre AutoCAD 2002 release will find the variables work the same way.

Offsetdist

Allows you to set a default value for the offset command. Type 'Offsetdist' and enter a new value in drawing units.

Advanced Drawing Commands

In this chapter, you'll learn how to use some of AutoCAD 2002's more advanced commands to create complex objects. Construction lines such as rays and xlines will help you to place objects on the drawing more accurately. They are designed to be quick to draw. Multilines and multiline styles are also treated in detail.

Covers

Chapter Four

Ray

How the command works

A ray is a line which has a starting point and extends off to infinity in a single direction. They are used to help construct a drawing rather than be objects as a part of the drawing. When the command is issued, AutoCAD 2002 will ask for the ray's starting point and then for another point through which the ray will run.

Command line: ray

Menu: Draw>Ray

Toolbar: (Doesn't appear by default – but can be customised)

The command in action

When the command is issued the response is:

Specify start point:	Select a point. You can use object snap or type an absolute co-ordinate
Specify through point:	Select a point.

Finish the command by pressing Enter or the Spacebar.

Rays emanating from a point. Rays have an endpoint for Object Snap but no midpoint.

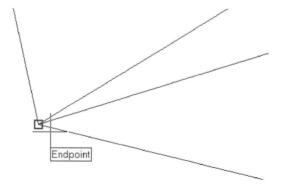

Endpoint

Construction Line or Xline

You can snap to the root of the xline using the Object Snap midpoint.

How the command works

A construction or xline is a line that runs to infinity in two directions. As in the construction of any type of line you need two points to define it. The first point you pick becomes the 'root' of the construction line. There are many ways to pick the points for constructing the xline, including the Object Snap modes.

Command line: xline, or the alias 'xl'

Menu: Draw>Construction Line

Toolbar:

The command in action

When the command is issued you have to select the first point or root. The default is to just pick a point on the screen or use Object Snap. Five other options are offered. To select one of these options type the capitalized letter from the list. The options are shown below:

Constructs a horizontal or vertical xline. Use Object Snap to draw it through a specific point.

Draws the xline parallel to an existing line – decide the distance

Specify a point or [Hor/Ver/Ang/Bisect/Offset]:

Use these construction lines sparingly, otherwise your drawing can quickly become cluttered with lines.

Specify an angle for the xline

Bisect an existing angle

Default option – just pick a point or use Object Snap

Then:

Through point: Select a point. You can use Object Snap or type a polar co-ordinate. Finish the command by pressing Enter or the Spacebar or click on the right mouse button.

Polylines

How the command works

Polylines are quite special. Unlike the standard line they can have a width and they can follow a curved path. Polylines need special editing options to modify them. To draw the polyline you need to give it a start and end point. Other options such as the width must be selected after the first point is chosen. You can give different widths for the beginning and end points of a polyline. AutoCAD 2002 will taper the line from one width to the other. Polylines can be turned into curves.

Command line: pline, or the alias 'pl'

Menu: Draw>Polyline

Toolbar:

The command in action

When the command is issued the response is:

Specify start point: Pick the first point

Current line width is 0.00

Specify next point or [Arc/Close/Halfwidth/Length/Undo/Width]:

If you right-click now the floating menu will appear with the list of options. You can pick one of these options instead of typing at the command line. Try it and pick the Width option. Enter a beginning width. Press Enter and type in an ending width. Try drawing a few lines.

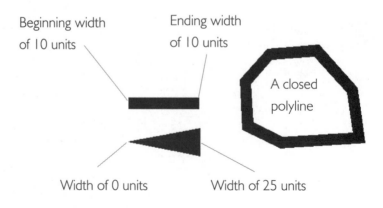

Beginning width of 10 units

Ending width of 10 units

A closed polyline

Width of 0 units

Width of 25 units

Polyline Shapes

Try turning the Fill option off by typing Fill at the command line and responding with 'off'.

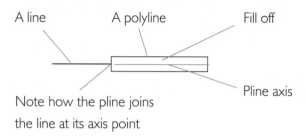

A line   A polyline   Fill off

Pline axis

Note how the pline joins the line at its axis point

Polylines can contain arcs. When you use the Arc option, select the arc endpoints and return to straight plines using the option 'l'.

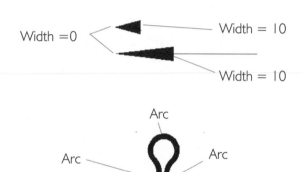

Width =0   Width = 10

Width = 10

Arc

Arc   Arc

Straight   Straight

The Length option allows a polyline to be increased by entering a value in units.

The prompt is 'Length of line:'

Just type a value and the line will be extended at the same angle as the existing polyline.

Fill can be on or off for all the polylines in the drawing. You cannot have some polylines with fill on and others with it off.

This shape was drawn with one execution of the command. The width was changed after each segment was drawn. The starting and ending width of each segment is the same.

Rectangles

How the command works

A rectangle is composed of four polylines. You simply pick two points to draw it. The sides of the rectangle are always parallel to the horizontal and vertical sides of the screen.

Command line: rectang

Menu: Draw>Rectangle

Toolbar:

The command in action

Issue the command. Pick two points:

Pick point 1

Pick point 2

3D Polyline and Rectangle

How the command works

3D polylines are similar to the standard pline. The differences are:

- they are drawn in 3D space and so can take a Z coordinate

- they can only be converted to special types of curves

Command line: pline, or the alias 'pl'

Menu: Draw>3DPolyline

Toolbar: None but can be customised

The command in action

When the command is issued the response is:

Specify start point of polyline: Pick as usual

Specify endpoint of line or [Undo]:

Donuts

If you erase a donut (or other object), it may appear that other parts of the drawing have also been erased. By typing 'r' for Redraw the screen is refreshed and you should see the unerased objects.

How the command works

Donuts are circles made from polylines. Donuts have two diameters. The area between the diameters is filled solid if the Fill command is set to On.

Command line: donut, or the alias 'do'

Menu: Draw>Donut

Toolbar: (Doesn't appear by default – but can be customised)

The command in action

You are simply asked for the inside and outside diameters. The default options are shown in angled brackets. The centre point can be picked using Object Snap or by just clicking on it. The Donut command will continue until Enter, the Spacebar or the right mouse button is pressed to finish it.

You must type 'Regen' after you change the Fill command. This allows you to see the effect on the donuts (or polylines).

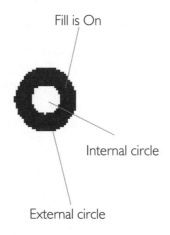

Fill is On

Internal circle

External circle

A donut with an inside diameter of 0 becomes a solid circle

Internal diameter is 0

Fill is Off

Splines

When experimenting with spline curves, use other drawing objects to snap on to. This will help you to remember the points you picked and consequently understand how the curves are formed.

How the command works

A spline is a curve. To create one, pick several points on-screen. AutoCAD 2002 will draw the curve through the first and last points, and as close as it can to those in between.

Command line: spline

Menu: Draw>Spline

Toolbar:

The command in action

You are asked for each point. Pick the points in the usual way and press enter three times to end the command. The splines below were drawn with different tolerances. To try it, draw two lines – one vertical and one horizontal.

Different Techniques

If the splines are not going the way you expect, check the tolerance setting.

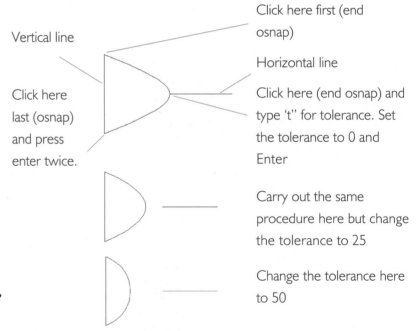

Vertical line

Click here last (osnap) and press enter twice.

Click here first (end osnap)

Horizontal line

Click here (end osnap) and type 't'' for tolerance. Set the tolerance to 0 and Enter

Carry out the same procedure here but change the tolerance to 25

Change the tolerance here to 50

AutoCAD 2002 will remember and use the last tolerance you set.

Notice how the spline always goes through the first and last point picked. It 'attempts' to go through the second point when the tolerance is above 0.

Ellipses

How the command works

An ellipse has a long (or major) axis and a short (or minor) axis. AutoCAD 2002 draws an ellipse by asking you to select or specify the length of the axis. Whichever is the longest is the major axis. In other words, you don't have to say which is major or minor: AutoCAD 2002 just lets you draw.

AutoCAD 2002 will take the longest axis as the major and the shorter one as the minor axis.

Command line: ellipse, or the alias 'el'

Menu: Draw>Ellipse

Toolbar:

The command in action

The command line default prompt is 'Specify axis endpoint of ellipse or [Arc/Center]:' Once the point is picked you have set the centre of the ellipse. The prompt now asks for you to 'Specify other endpoint of axis'. This will determine the length of the first axis. The prompt for 'Specify distance to other axis or [Rotation]:' describes the ellipse fully.

The length of the axis can be input as polar co-ordinates.

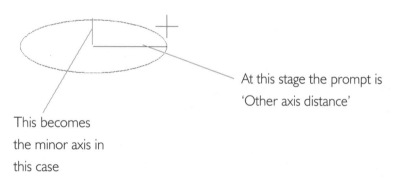

At this stage the prompt is 'Other axis distance'

This becomes the minor axis in this case

The 'Center' option allows you to pick the centre of the ellipse first. You then need to tell AutoCAD 2002 the length of the axes.

If you draw in isometric mode you can create isocircles. These are really ellipses pretending to be circles viewed at an angle.

Arcs

How the command works

There are many ways to draw an arc. AutoCAD 2002 has 10 ways listed on the drop-down menu. Arcs are parts of circles. All arcs have a beginning and an end point. AutoCAD 2002 uses these points in three techniques. All arcs have a centre; this is used in six techniques. Three techniques use the idea of an angle to specify the distance the arc spans.

Arcs are made from a circle. Three points are needed for AutoCAD 2002 to draw the arc.

Command line: arc

Menu: Draw>Arc

Toolbar:

Arc Options

3 Points
Start, Center, End
Start, Center, Angle
Start, End, Angle
Center, Start, End
Center, Start, Angle
Continue

The command in action

Here are two techniques:

1 The Start, Center, End option.

Start, Center, End

The arc is drawn in an anticlockwise direction

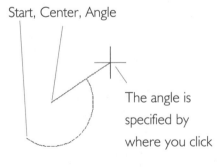

Arcs can be a bit difficult to master. Concentrate on one (perhaps the Start Center, End) until you can predict the results.

2 The Start, Center, Angle option.

Start, Center, Angle

Negative angles give a clockwise arc

The angle is specified by where you click

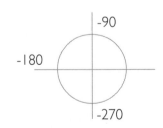

How to Draw a Door Arc

This is the type of arc that is used by an architect to describe the sweep of a door.

An angle that is negative sweeps an arc clockwise.

To follow this, set up a drawing using decimal units, with a sheet size of about 2000mm by 2000mm. Use double lines to draw a wall and a single line to represent the door at 90 degrees to the wall. The door gap must also be 900mm. The arc will be drawn using the option Start, Center, Angle.

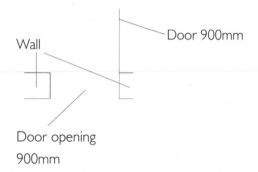

Wall

Door 900mm

Door opening
900mm

Use the Object Snap modes to position the arc Start and Center points.

Command sequence

Pick Start, Center, Angle from the Draw>Arc menu.

Pick the start point using Object Snap End to locate the top of the door.

The Angle option is used to describe the distance the arc sweeps.

For the centre pick where the door meets the wall using Object Snap Midpoint.

When asked for the angle type in 90. This sweeps an arc anticlockwise through a distance of 90 degrees.

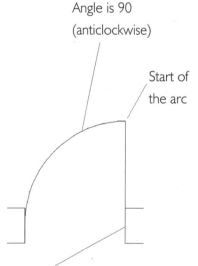

Angle is 90
(anticlockwise)

Start of
the arc

Centre of the circle that makes the
arc Mid point

Multilines

This command allows you to draw between 1 and 16 lines parallel to each other. You must tell AutoCAD the distance between the parallel lines. In the examples below, the command is illustrated with the default of two parallel lines.

Command line: mline, or the alias ml

Menu: Draw>Multiline

Toolbar:

Once the command is issued, AutoCAD responds with:

Current settings: Justification=Top,Scale=20,Style=STANDARD

Specify start point or [Justification/Scale/STyle]:

Scale is the distance in units between the parallel lines. Justification determines where the start point of a vertex is. Both these settings are illustrated in the diagram below. TOP, ZERO and BOTTOM refer to the justification. The scale is 6.

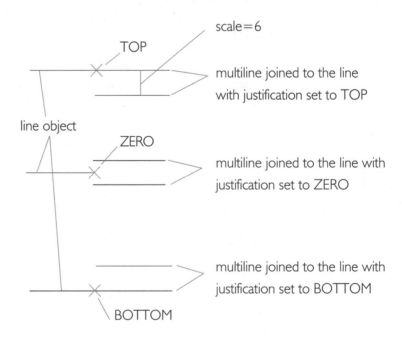

...cont'd

Multilines can be closed to form enclosed shapes. A closed multiline automatically joins the beginning and end of the shape. When you are drawing a multiline shape, the command option 'c' closes the shape, otherwise just press Enter to finish the command.

Multilines will not trim or extend with these commands. You have to use the special editing command Mledit.

A closed multiline

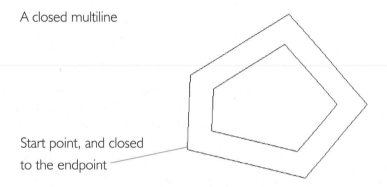

Start point, and closed
to the endpoint

If a multiline is selected for further editing, the complete multiline drawn in one command session will be highlighted (similar to a polyline). To edit the multiline you can explode it with

from the Modify toolbar. This will return it to individual lines, each of which can be edited in the normal way.

Editing Multilines

How the command works

Because multilines consist of at least two parallel lines, there are many types of intersections available when they cross or meet. The 'mledit' command allows you to edit these intersection points. The command opens the Multiline Edit Tools box. From this you apply the type of intersection you want.

Command line: mledit

Menu: Modify>Object>Multiline

Toolbar: 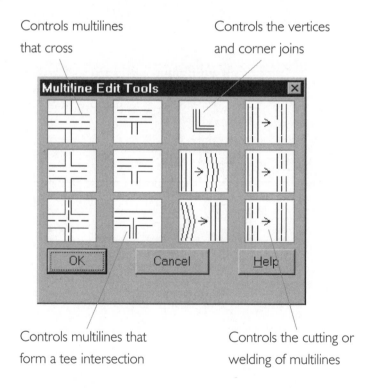 (found on the Modify II toolbar)

The command in action

When the command is issued, the Multiline Edit Tools dialogue box is displayed. The box is divided into four columns. Each column helps you to edit a different type of intersection.

Controls multilines that cross

Controls the vertices and corner joins

Controls multilines that form a tee intersection

Controls the cutting or welding of multilines

Examples of Multiline Editing

The Closed Cross

In this first example the two multilines are intersecting in the default manner.

1 Issue the 'mledit' command; AutoCAD will display the Multiline Edit Tools dialogue box.

2 Select the top left option 'Closed Cross' and click OK.

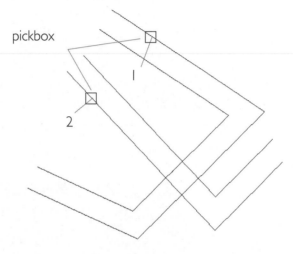

pickbox

1

2

All the other editing options work in a similar way.

3 AutoCAD will now ask you to select the 'first mline'. Select the one you want to 'dominate' or run over the second one. In this case pick 1 in the illustration.

4 In response to 'second mline' pick at point 2 in the illustration.

The first multiline now 'dominates' the second at the point of intersection

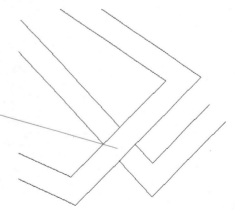

Creating Multiline Styles

The description can be up to 255 characters.

Multiline styles help you to control how a multiline looks when drawn. For example, a style may be set up for a multiline to have four parallel lines with a specified offset between each one. You may decide to apply a different colour or linetype to each line in the multiline. Multilines may also have the ends capped. All of these elements can be saved as a multiline style.

To create a new style, follow the steps below:

1 Run the Multiline Style command: Format>Multiline Style...

2 The Multiline Styles dialogue box is displayed.

3 Click in the 'Name' box and type in the name of a new style you want to create. In this case, type in FOUR.

4 Type in a description of the style you are creating. This description is for the user.

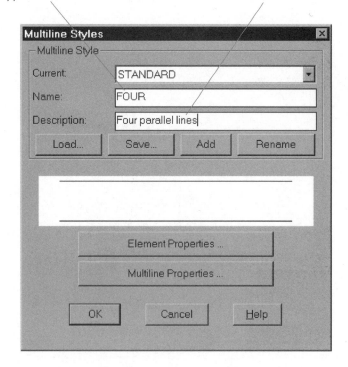

...cont'd

5 Click on Add to make the style current. You can then proceed to develop this style.

6 Click on Element Properties to define the elements of the multiline that make its new style. The Element Properties dialogue box is displayed.

The offset distance is measured from the central axis of the
multiline.

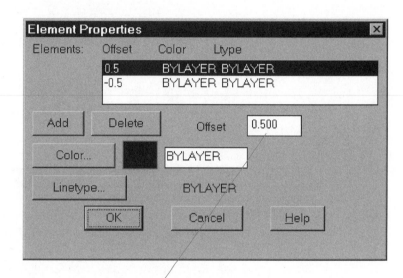

You can add up to 16 elements to a multiline style.

7 Select Offset, type in a new value (say 0.5) and press Enter. Click on Add. This will create another parallel line. Repeat it for an offset value of 1 (don't forget to click Add again). This will create two parallel lines. The offset distance is from the central axis of the multiline.

8 Try changing the colour of one of the lines in the multiline by clicking on 'Color'.

9 Assign a linetype by clicking on Linetype. You will probably need to Load a new linetype.

10 Click OK when you've finished. This returns you to the Multiline Styles dialogue. Click OK; try drawing a multiline.

Modifying Multiline Properties

Open the Multiline Style dialogue box: Format>Multiline Style...

You cannot change the properties of an existing multiline – you will have to rename it and then make modifications.

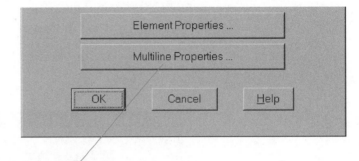

Click on Multiline Properties to open a dialogue box which allows you to add end caps to multilines, or to add a fill. After you have made changes, click on OK.

The joints appear at the vertices

Controls the multiline endings

Click here to add a fill to the lines

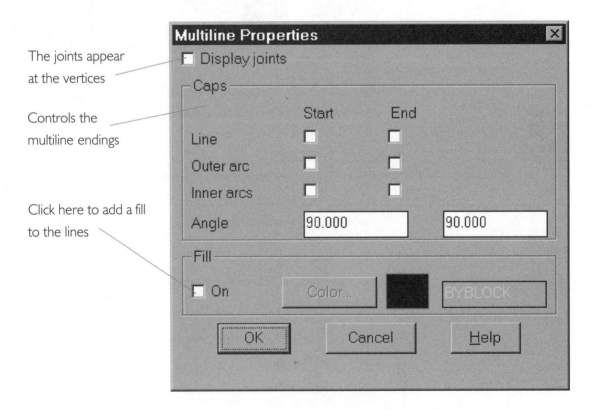

A Library of Multiline Styles

Saving a style

Styles can be saved to a file with the extension MLN. A MLN file stores styles added to it. Click on Save in the Multiline Styles dialogue box (Format>Multiline Styles) after you have created a style. The Save Multiline Style dialogue box appears. Enter a name and click OK.

You cannot edit the STANDARD multiline style.

The default file that holds the STANDARD style

File name

Leave '.mln' as the file extension

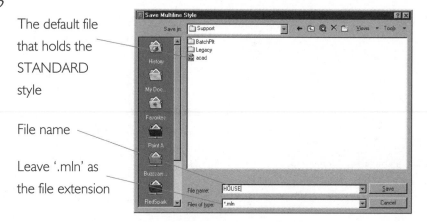

To use a multiline style, select Load from the Multiline Styles Dialogue box.

The multiline style here has a colour fill with an arc endcap, and the joints are displayed

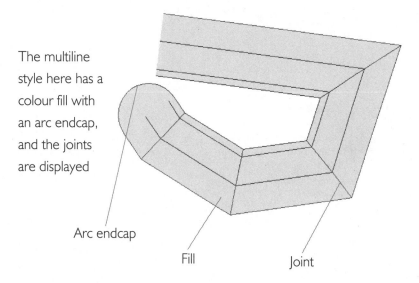

Arc endcap

Fill

Joint

Arcs by default join the outer elements of the multiline.

Polygons

Polygons are made from polylines. You can edit them using the pedit command.

How the command works

A polygon is an enclosed shape with 3 to 1024 sides. You can draw a polygon in two basic ways. Define one side of the polygon and AutoCAD 2002 will draw the others or pick the centre of the polygon and AutoCAD 2002 will draw the sides inside or outside a circle.

Command line: polygon

Menu: Draw>Polygon

Toolbar:

The command in action

You can Object Snap a line onto the mid point or end point of the sides of the polyline.

Issue the command. AutoCAD will want to know the number of sides in the polygon. Type in a value and press enter. The response is:

Specify center of polygon or [Edge]: pick a point

Enter option [Inscribed in circle/Circumscribed about circle]<I>:

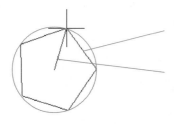

This is an inscribed 5 sided polygon

The radius can be input as a value or picked with the cursor

Even though a polygon can be defined around or inside a circle, you cannot Object Snap to the centre of a polygon.

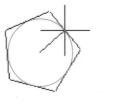

This is a circumscribed 5 sided polygon

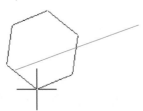

This is a 5 sided polygon from a straight edge

Isometric Drawing

In this chapter, you'll learn how to produce isometric drawings using the isometric setup procedure. You will move from one isoplane to another. The use of viewports is illustrated with its application to isometric drawing. Lastly, you will place some text on each of the isoplanes.

Covers

Chapter Five

Isometric Drawing

AutoCAD 2002 lets you produce two-dimensional isometric drawings (30/60) with ease. Isometric drawings are not three-dimensional. The image you produce is strictly on a two-dimensional plane, as it would be if it were a traditional hand-drawing on paper.

Isometric drawings are flat. They cannot be rotated to see what is behind them.

The Isometric mode

To execute a drawing in Isometric mode, you must first select the isometric style and then select the isoplane that you will work on.

The drawing below is produced in Isometric mode. It has three planes. To produce a drawing like this you must toggle from one plane to another. In this drawing, the top plane is shown to be active. This is confirmed by the orientation of the crosshairs:

An isometric drawing is NOT a 3D drawing.

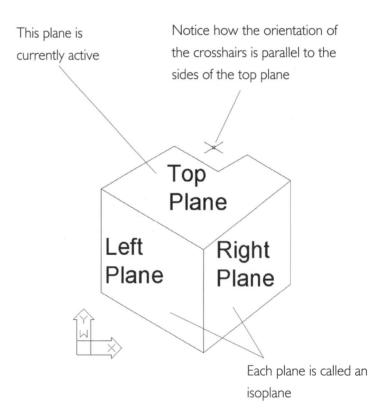

This plane is currently active

Notice how the orientation of the crosshairs is parallel to the sides of the top plane

Top Plane

Left Plane

Right Plane

Each plane is called an isoplane

Setting Up the Isometric Mode

To execute a drawing in Isometric mode you must first make the mode active. Then you need to set the isoplane you want to draw on as current. To do this, follow the steps below:

1   From the Tools menu select Drafting Settings...

 You can select an isoplane by typing 'isoplane' at the command line and pressing Enter.

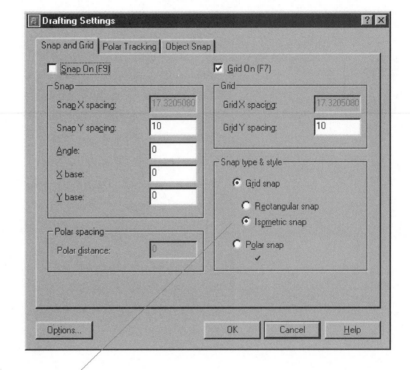

 Text set with an orientation of 0 degrees will remain horizontal.

2   In the Drafting Settings dialogue box, activate the Isometric Snap/ Grid by checking 'On'.

3   Switch on the grid if it is not already on.

Notice the orientation of the crosshairs. As you draw you will need to toggle from one isoplane to another. To do this, press the F5 function key or use Ctrl+E.

An Isometric Shape

The best way to understand how to put an isometric drawing together is to draw a shape similar to that on page 62, which uses the three isoplanes top, left and right. Follow the steps below:

1 Press the F5 function key or the Ctrl+E combination until the Left Isoplane is current.

Pressing the F5 function key toggles between isoplanes.

2 Make sure that the Snap is on. You can check this by looking at the status line at the bottom of the screen. Notice the shape of the crosshairs – they follow the line of the Left Isoplane. Draw the shape as it appears here.

3 Switch to the Top Isoplane by pressing the F5 function key, or Ctrl+E. Again notice the orientation of the crosshairs. Draw the top plane as shown.

4 Press the F5 function key to switch to the Right Isoplane and draw the rest of the shape as shown.

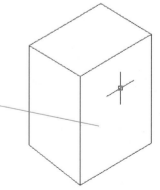

Drawing an Isocircle

To draw a circle in Isometric mode you must use the ellipse command. The ellipse command has an 'isocircle' option. Using this option, we will apply a circle to the isoplanes of the shape drawn on the previous page. (Note that the standard 'circle' command will not work in Isometric mode.)

First select the isoplane you want to place the circle on. Then, issue the ellipse command. The options displayed are:

Specify axis endpoint of ellipse or [Arc/Center/Isocircle]:

Right-click the mouse button and select Isocircle from the floating menu. Select the location for the centre of the circle. Issue the radius or diameter of the circle. The circle will be drawn to look correct on the isoplane.

The illustration below shows isocircles placed on the three isoplanes of the shape:

The isocircle option within the ellipse command is available in Isometric mode only.

The normal 'circle' command will not put a correct circle on an isoplane.

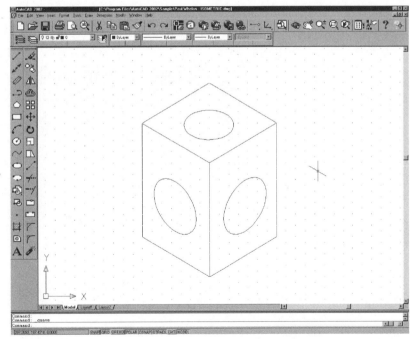

Isometric Drawing and Viewports

Viewports can speed up the isometric drawing process considerably. This is done by setting up three viewports with a different isoplane active in each port. You should then save the viewport configuration.

During the drawing process you simply click in the viewport which displays the isoplane you want to draw on.

Setting up the viewports

Follow these steps to set up three viewports and assign each one to an isoplane:

1   Start a New drawing in the usual way. If you have the isometric shape drawn (see earlier), then you can use that.

2   From the View drop-down menu, select Viewports.

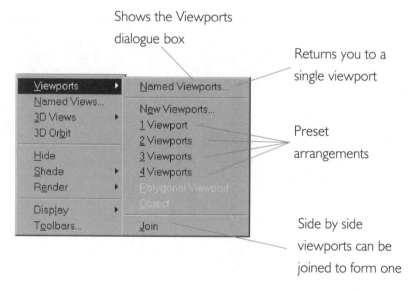

Shows the Viewports dialogue box

Returns you to a single viewport

Preset arrangements

Side by side viewports can be joined to form one

3   Click on New Viewports... The screen on the facing page is displayed.

The Active Model Configuration shows the current setup (this one is a single viewport).

Above & Below refer to which viewport will be the largest

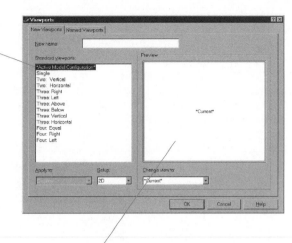

4 Select 'Three: Above'. The Preview screen will divide into three tiled viewports, each one showing the same view of the drawing. Click on OK.

5 Move the crosshairs from one viewport to another and the crosshairs will change to an arrow. The active or current viewport is the one with the crosshairs. To make another viewport active just click in it.

You cannot have a different drawing in each viewport.

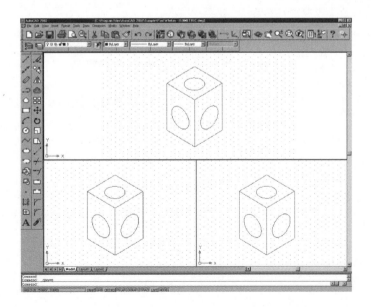

To return to a single viewport, select the View drop-down menu, then Single Viewport. The view that appears in the single port is the current or active one.

6 When a viewport is active you can draw and edit in it in the normal way.

7 Each viewport can have a different setting for the zoom level. A different isoplane can be assigned now to each viewport. The image below shows three different levels of zoom:

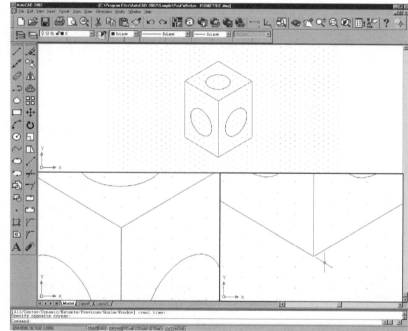

Commands can be started in one viewport and continued in another. Try drawing a line from one to another. Remember that you start the command in an active viewport and when you move to the inactive port you must click first to make it active.

To set up the isoplanes

1 Make the top viewport current and press F5 until it is assigned the 'top' isoplane.

2 Make the left viewport current and press F5 until it is assigned the 'left' isoplane. Carry out the same procedure for the right isoplane.

Saving/Restoring Tiled Viewports

Once the viewports are arranged suitably, you can save the configuration. This will allow you to return to the same arrangement whenever the drawing is opened again. The restore option allows you to restore a pre-saved arrangement.

Saving an arrangement

Saving and restoring viewports can speed up work on large complex drawings.

1 Set up an arrangement of tiled viewports.

2 From the View drop-down menu, select Viewports and then New Viewports.

3 Make sure this is highlighted and this is the current configuration you want to save.

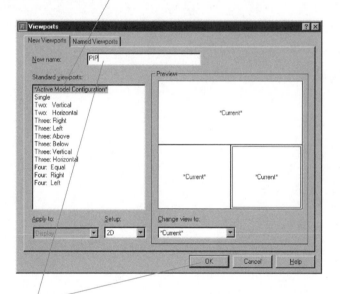

4 Type in a name and click on OK. This saves the viewport arrangement.

5 To Restore this named viewport arrangement use the View>Viewports>Named Viewports menu option and you will see the name you have given to the viewports arrangement. Click on it to restore it.

Text on Isometric Drawings

If you place text on an isometric drawing with a rotation angle of zero (0), it will run parallel to the bottom of the page.

The top isoplane will look equally well with -30 or +30 degree text.

You can run the text parallel to the 'bottom' of an isoplane by using the following rotation angles:

- Top Isoplane text rotation angle is 30 degrees.

- Left Isoplane text rotation angle is -30 degrees.

- Right Isoplane text rotation angle is 30 degrees.

These are shown in the illustration below:

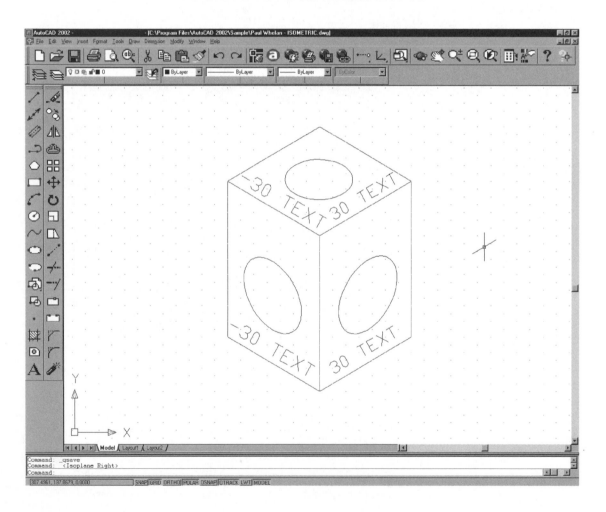

Pseudo-3D Drawing

In this chapter, you'll learn how to produce pseudo-3D drawings – the Z Dimension – using the elevation and thickness command. You will also learn to view the drawing from different positions, above and below the object. The limitations associated with the elevation command are also described.

Covers

Chapter Six

Not really 2D Drawing!

All the 2D drawing you have done up to now has been done in a 3D environment. In other words, AutoCAD 2002 treats a 2D drawing as though it is 3D, but with the coordinates of the Z axis kept at 0.

The icon at the bottom left of the screen is called the World Coordinate System icon.

With this idea in mind, set up an A3 sheet (420★297) in decimal units. Draw a simple shape to represent two rooms with an opening for the door (don't worry about the dimensions as this is just an illustration).

The icons at the bottom left of the screen show the direction of the X and Y axes. The Z axis projects up from your computer screen towards you, at 90 degrees to the plane formed by the X and Y axes.

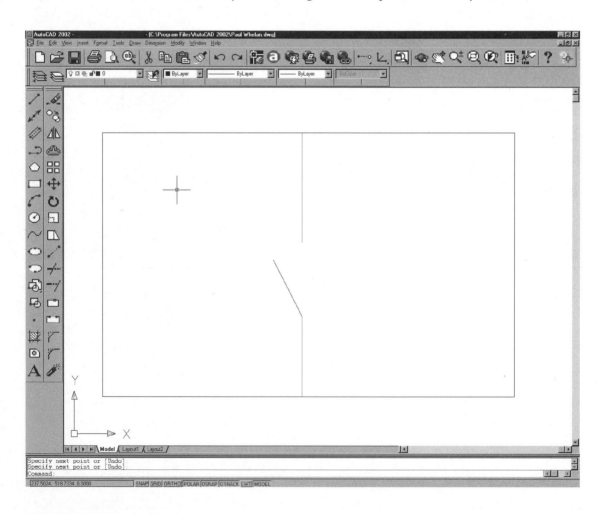

In other words you are looking straight down the Z axis at the drawing in plan view. To view the drawing from another angle, try the following steps:

1   From the View menu select 3D Views.

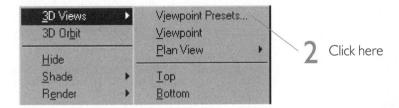

2   Click here

There is also a command called DVIEW which will allow you to position your viewpoint above or below the drawing dynamically.

3   The Viewpoint Presets dialogue box appears. From this, select your position in space from which to view the drawing.

4   Click here to be 45 degrees behind the drawing.

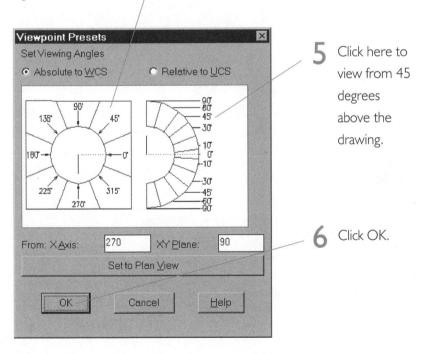

5   Click here to view from 45 degrees above the drawing.

6   Click OK.

The Z axis is at 90 degrees to the X–Y plane that the drawing is on.

AutoCAD 2002 will display this view of the drawing. Examine the World Coordinate System icon; this will help you to understand that you are behind the object and above it.

The negative Z axis drops below the plane of the drawing.

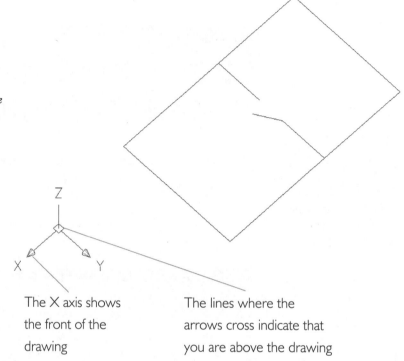

The X axis shows the front of the drawing

The lines where the arrows cross indicate that you are above the drawing

To define a viewpoint without using the preset views, you must input a view angle above (or below) the object and behind (or in front of) it.

If the UCS icon does not look like the one displayed here, see page 138 on how to change its display style to 2D flat view.

Thickness – the Z dimension

This drawing has no third dimension because the Z axis thickness is 0. Now you will change the properties of the lines that make up the drawing by giving them a thickness of 100 units.

1 Without issuing a command, pull a window over the whole drawing. Little blue boxes called grips will appear on the midpoints and endpoints of the lines.

2 From the Modify drop down menu select Properties...

A negative value will extrude the drawing below the X–Y plane.

3 The Properties dialogue box is displayed.

4 Change the 'Thickness' value to 100 and press Enter.

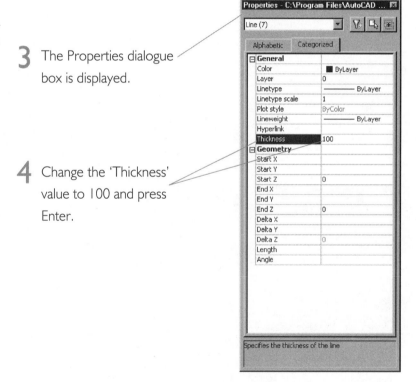

Properties - C:\Program Files\AutoCAD ...		
Line (7)		
Alphabetic	Categorized	
General		
Color	■ ByLayer	
Layer	0	
Linetype	—— ByLayer	
Linetype scale	1	
Plot style	ByColor	
Lineweight	—— ByLayer	
Hyperlink		
Thickness	100	
Geometry		
Start X		
Start Y		
Start Z	0	
End X		
End Y		
End Z	0	
Delta X		
Delta Y		
Delta Z	0	
Length		
Angle		

Specifies the thickness of the line

All the lines of the drawing will extrude up the Z axis. Because the viewpoint you set was above the drawing at an angle of 45 degrees, the 3D effect should be obvious. Close the Properties dialogue box by clicking on the X icon in the top right-hand corner. See the next page.

Press the Esc key twice
to remove the grips
from the display

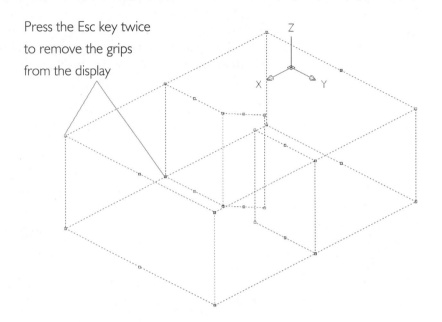

Try setting up other views of the drawing. Here is a further
example of the drawing viewed from the front but underneath
(negative Z axis).

315 degrees from
the X axis

-60 degrees in the
XY plane

Note: the Z axis is a
dotted line. This indicates
that you are viewing the
object from underneath

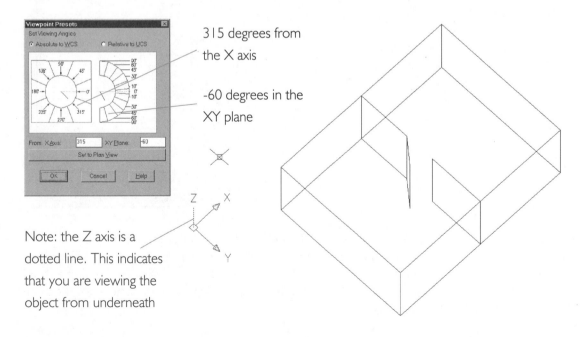

Using Hide

In the drawings on the previous few pages you can see through the object as though the sides were made of glass. The Hide command will allow you to see the object as though the sides were opaque. To issue the Hide command, type 'hide' at the command prompt and press Enter. AutoCAD will regenerate the drawing without the lines behind objects.

You cannot continue editing and drawing in Hide mode.

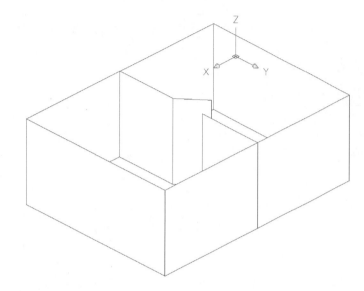

To leave Hide mode you must type Regen and press Enter.

This is the drawing you viewed from underneath (page 76) after Hide has been issued

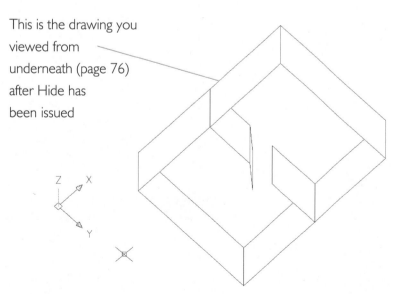

The Drawing/Editing Commands

All the standard drawing and editing commands will work on a drawing with a thickness on the Z axis (positive or negative). Be careful, however, as they only work on the X–Y plane. You will not be able to copy an object up the Z axis until you have a better understanding of true 3D drawing.

The drawing below had the walls offset by 10 units and the corners filleted with a radius of 10 units. Try applying these commands while in the view looking down on the shape.

Copying or moving objects will only take place on the current elevation. The current elevation is also the X–Y plane.

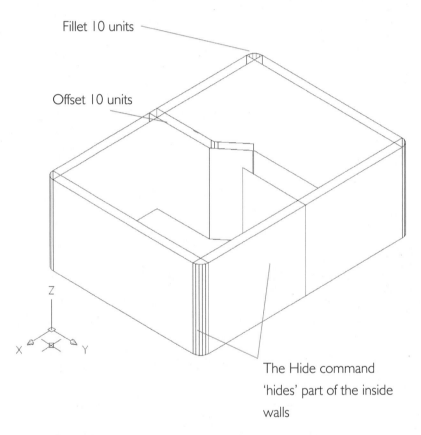

Fillet 10 units

Offset 10 units

The Hide command 'hides' part of the inside walls

The fillet command places a fillet arc at the corners. This is shown in 3D AutoCAD with vertical lines called tessellations.

Elevation and Thickness

Elevation is the level up or down the Z axis at which you draw or edit. For example, in the previous drawing an elevation of 30 allows you to draw at the height of the walls. The thickness that you set will extrude the object from the elevation you are working at.

Elevation and thickness with circles

Start a new drawing. Again, use an A3 sheet (see page 8 for the dimensions) with decimal units. Then follow these steps to understand the elevation settings:

1. To set the elevation to 30, first type 'elev' at the command prompt and press Enter. Make sure the elevation value is zero. This means that you are drawing on the X–Y plane as you would in a standard 2D drawing. Press Enter.

2. AutoCAD advises you on a thickness. Type 25 and press Enter.

3. Next, issue the circle command. Pick the 'center point' near the centre of the screen and put in a radius of 50 units.

4. Issue the elev command again and set the value to 25 (the height of the circle).

5. Draw a second circle inside the first with a radius of 12 units.

6. Change your view of the drawing to 315 degrees from the X axis and 10 degrees from the X–Y plane. Your drawing should look similar to that below when you issue the hide command.

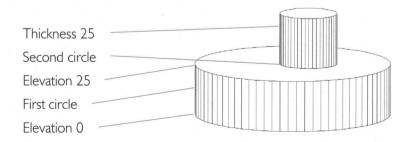

Thickness 25

Second circle

Elevation 25

First circle

Elevation 0

Thickness Limitations

To produce a 3D model, you will first need to read chapters 12–15.

Drawing with thickness and elevation is not considered true 3D drawing. To understand why, look at the steps involved in the production of a 3D model. Do as follows (but see the HOT TIP in the margin first):

- Draw a wireframe model

- Place faces on the wireframe

- Render the faces

The opaque sides of a shape produced by the thickness command are not 'faces'. You cannot place a texture (such as stone or wood) on them. This immediately limits their use in a full 3D drawing. It prevents you from rendering the 'faces' to produce wood or stone effects.

It is also impossible to edit objects with a thickness to place, say, an opening such as a window in them.

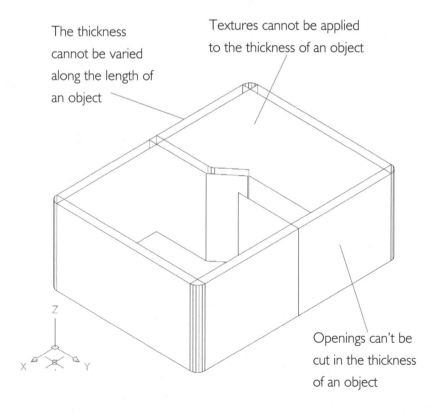

The thickness cannot be varied along the length of an object

Textures cannot be applied to the thickness of an object

Openings can't be cut in the thickness of an object

Text and Units

In this chapter, you'll learn how to place text on a drawing. Editing of the text, including the use of the Spell Checker, is also treated. The old problem of selecting a text size for plotting/printing is also tackled. And lastly, we will look at how you can control the setup and display of units in the Drawing Units dialogue box.

Covers

Chapter Seven

Using Single Line Text

Introduction to text commands

Text is very important in precision drawings such as those produced by AutoCAD 2002. Text is an object on a drawing, just as a line or a circle is an object. This implies that it is open to the same editing commands such as Scale, Move and Erase. AutoCAD 2002 allows you to use many different styles of text. You can also create a style yourself from the given fonts.

Text is an entity that can be scaled, moved, mirrored, etc., like any other entity.

Single Line Text

At times you will need to just put a line of text on the drawing for the purpose of annotation. For this you use the Single Line Text command. If you need to place several lines of text on the drawing use the Multiline Text editor.

How the command works

AutoCAD 2002 will ask you to click on a start point for the text. A cursor will display at that point. You then type the text and press Enter to move to the next line or Enter again to finish the command. The options available allow you to justify the text (left, right or centre) or apply a style. Once a point is selected you must supply the text height and the angle of orientation.

Command: dtext, or the alias 'dt'

Menu: Draw>Text>Single Line Text

The command in action

Pressing the Spacebar inserts a space in the 'Text' option. Normally in AutoCAD 2002 it is the equivalent of pressing the Enter key.

Issue the Single Line Text command. Select a start point. Enter a height. This height can be picked with the cursor. AutoCAD 2002 will offer you the last height you used as the default. A rotation angle of 0 means the text is horizontal. At the prompt 'Text', type in the text you want. This is one of the few cases where pressing the Spacebar will put in a space and won't be construed as Enter.

Standard text font

Using single line text

Start or insertion point

Paragraph Text

The first time this command is run, AutoCAD 2002 has to 'initialise' the editor. This may take a few seconds, so be patient.

How the command works

Use this text option to place several lines of text in a drawing. When the command is issued you will be asked to specify the corners of a box. The text you type will fill the box. AutoCAD 2002 opens a small word processor for you to enter and edit the text.

Command: mtext, or the alias 'mt'

Menu: Draw>Text>Multiline Text

Toolbar: A

The command in action

Issue the Paragraph Text command. Pick a 'first' and 'opposite' corner to show AutoCAD 2002 where you want the text positioned. The Multiline Text Editor opens:

The current font

Click here for other fonts

Font size

Holds special characters, like the degree or diameter symbol

Type in here

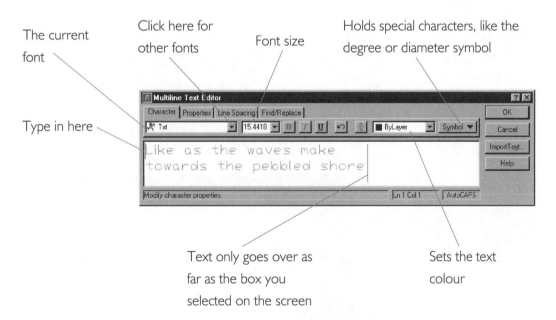

Text only goes over as far as the box you selected on the screen

Sets the text colour

Click on OK when you have finished with the editor.

Multiline Text Editor Options

The style option under the Properties tab will contain the STANDARD style only, unless you have already defined some styles yourself.

The Character, Properties and Find/Replace tabs lead into many options within the Multiline Text Editor. The Properties tab is shown below.

Positions text within the box. Select the text by dragging over it and then select a Justification option

Allows you to change the width of the text box

The Rich Text Format (rtf) retains the formatting of text and is available under Save As in most word processors.

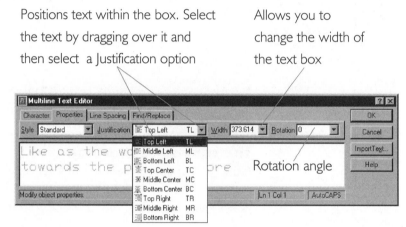

Rotation angle

Click Import Text to import a text document written outside AutoCAD 2002.

When the Import Text button is selected, the 'Select File' dialogue box is displayed to allow you to look through folders for the text file. Most word processors can save files in rtf (Rich Text Format). This is a good format to use for files which you want to import into AutoCAD 2002.

Click the folder here

You can only import files up to 16K in size.

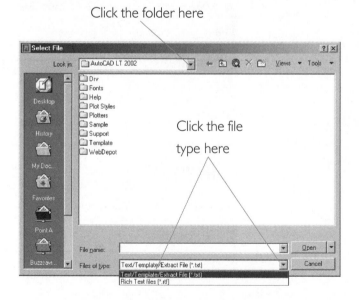

Click the file type here

The Spell Checker

The Spell Checker can be called up by typing 'spell' or the alias 'sp' at the command line.

The Spell Checker is found under the Tools drop-down menu.

Menu: Tools>Spelling

Toolbar:

The suggested word. If this is not correct, type the word here or pick it from the list below

Ignore all cases of the word

The Check Spelling dialogue box will only appear if there is a misspelling in the text you have selected.

Check Spelling   ✕

Current dictionary: British English (ise)

Current word

theee

Cancel

Help

Suggestions:

the

| the |
| they |
| them |
| theme |
| then |
| there |

Ignore   Ignore All

Change   Change All

Add   Lookup

Change Dictionaries...

Context

theee

The sentence selected on the drawing for checking

Adds the word into the dictionary so it will be recognised the next time

Offers American and British dictionaries

Editing Text

Command line: ddedit, or the alias 'ed'

Menu: Modify>Text

Icon: 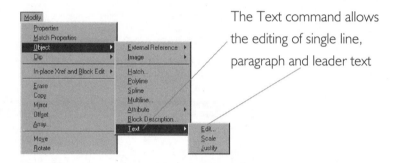 on the Modify II toolbar

The Text command allows
the editing of single line,
paragraph and leader text

*The Multiline
Text Editor will
only open if the
text was
originally
inserted using the Paragraph
Text command.*

If the text you selected was created by the Single
Line Text command (dtext), this text editor will
appear. Simple editing can be performed

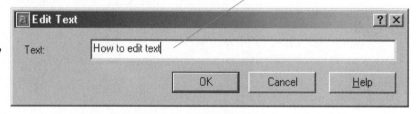

*Text in the
Multiline Text
Editor can be
modified in the
usual way,
including changing font or
style, etc.*

If the text you selected was created by the
Paragraph Text command (mtext), the Multiline
Text Editor will open with the selected text

The selected text is
loaded into the editor

Text Size and Plotting/Printing

If you are unsure at what scale the drawing will be printed, input the text as though the plot will be 1:100. Changing the text size to 1:25, or 1:250 is then easy.

When you are selecting text height for a drawing, you must try and keep in mind the scale that the drawing will eventually be plotted at. Because text is often the only object on a drawing that does not represent something in the real world, it is not placed on the drawing in real world size.

Text size on a plotted drawing

To find out the size the text will be on the printed drawing you must divide the text height by the plot scale. For example:

Text height input   =   500mm

Drawing plotted   =   1:100

Text height on the plotted drawing is 500/100 = 5mm

The phrase 'plot scale' is the scale the drawing is printed at. If you print at 1:50, then 50 is the plot scale.

And vice versa, if the text must be 8mm high on a drawing at 1:250, the calculation is:

8*250 =   2000mm

Some other examples

- 4mm text is input as 400mm on a 1:100 plot.

- 5mm text is input as 250mm on a 1:50 plot.

- 6mm text is input as 150mm on a 1:25 plot.

Text for signs on a drawing will be shown in real-world size and consequently must be input in real-world size just as any other object in the drawing.

Multiply the height you want the text to be on the printed drawing by the scale factor it is printed at, to find out what size you enter the text at.

Controlling the Drawing Units

The units can be changed at any time during the drawing process.

How the command works
The Drawing Units dialogue box allows you to change the type of drawing units and their precision.

Command line: ddunits

Menu: Format>Units

The command in action
Issue the Units command. The Drawing Units dialogue is displayed.

Select the drawing units here

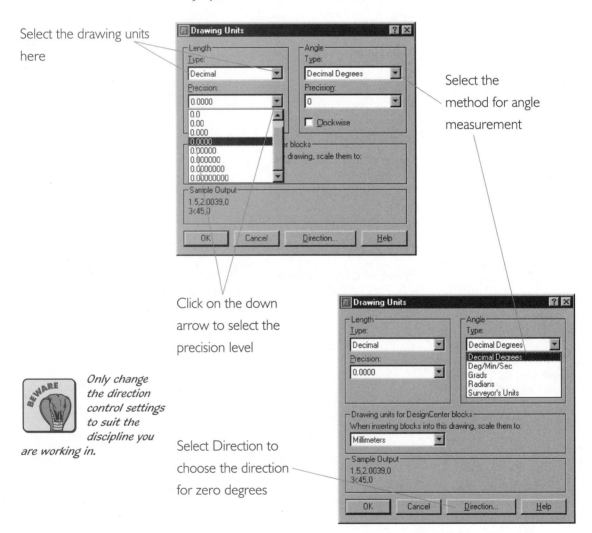

Select the method for angle measurement

Click on the down arrow to select the precision level

Only change the direction control settings to suit the discipline you are working in.

Select Direction to choose the direction for zero degrees

Editing Techniques

In this chapter, you'll learn to use important editing commands such as Offset, Trim and Extend. All the commands selected for this chapter are used frequently by AutoCAD users in all disciplines. For example, there are few drawings where the Offset command would not be used.

Covers

Chapter Eight

Offset

Polylines are offset from the axis that runs down through the centre of the pline.

How the command works

Offset will make a copy of objects parallel to existing objects. It is one of the most useful commands in AutoCAD 2002 and is well worth mastering. You will be asked what you want to offset and then the distance to offset and finally the side of the original object you want the offset to occur on.

Command line: offset

Menu: Modify>Offset

Toolbar: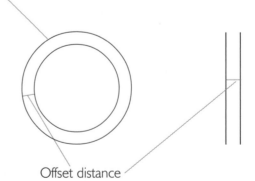

The command in action

AutoCAD 2002 keeps the last offset distance as the default.

Issue the Offset command. AutoCAD 2002 immediately asks for the distance you want to offset – 'Specify offset distance or [Through] <Through>:' Enter a distance and select the object. You can only select one object to offset at a time. Finally select the side to offset the object.

If you offset a polyline make sure that the offset distance is more than the halfwidth distance of the polyline, otherwise you won't see it.

The inner circle was produced by offsetting the outer one by 10 units

The left line was offset by 10 units on the right

Offset distance

Rotate

How the command works

You can rotate any objects around a central rotation point. Select the objects to rotate, then specify the base point about which the rotation is to occur (which can be on the object itself) and lastly the angle through which the rotation should occur. A positive rotation angle means anticlockwise. A negative angle is clockwise.

Rotate is a grip option. Highlight a grip and press the Spacebar until you see Rotate.

Command line: rotate, or the alias 'ro'

Menu: Modify>Rotate

Toolbar:

The command in action

Issue the Rotate command. AutoCAD will tell you what the current settings are (direction of angle measurement etc. as specified in the ddunits command).

Select the objects and press Enter to finish the selection. You can mix the selection methods. Now AutoCAD 2002 will ask 'Specify base point:'. Pick a point. Type a value in response to the prompt for 'Specify a rotation angle or [Reference]:'.

The reference angle allows a rotation from some existing angle – usually of the object being rotated.

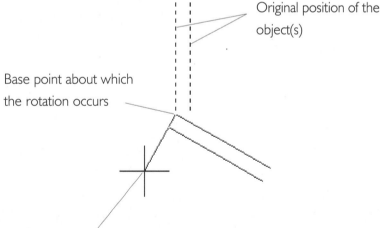

Original position of the object(s)

Base point about which the rotation occurs

The cursor is attached to this base point. As it is moved the objects rotate. Type an angle if you like or just click on a point on the screen

Stretch

How the command works

The Stretch command lengthens or shortens objects. A crossing window or polygon must cross the objects you want to stretch. Any object which lies completely within the selection window is moved. AutoCAD 2002 will ask you for a base point, to calculate the amount of stretch.

Command line: Stretch

Menu: Modify>Stretch

Toolbar:

The command in action

Issue the Stretch command. Select the objects by pulling a crossing window or polygon so that it cuts or crosses them .

Select objects: Pull a crossing window or crossing polygon

Specify base point   Pick a point on/near the object
or displacement:

Second point of displacement: Click on a point with the cursor or use co-ordinates or Object Snap to another object

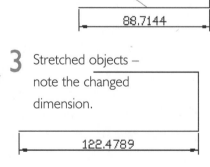

1 Lines to be stretched.

88.7144

3 Stretched objects – note the changed dimension.

122.4789

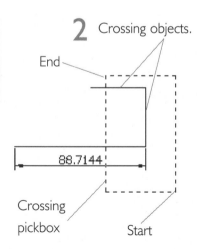

2 Crossing objects.

End

88.7144

Crossing pickbox

Start

Lengthen

If an object is closed – like a double line or a polyline – it cannot be lengthened.

How the command works

This command will allow you to increase or decrease the length of objects. Basically you just select the objects and then tell AutoCAD 2002 how you want to increase/decrease the length of the objects. There are several very interesting options. You can lengthen the object by a percent or by a specific amount. You may also give AutoCAD 2002 an overall length for a object and it will modify the object to suit that length.

Command line: lengthen, or the alias 'len'

Menu: Modify>Lengthen

Toolbar:

The command in action

You can use lengthen to find the existing length of an object. Issue the command and select the object. AutoCAD 2002 will tell you its length.

To try this command with the Delta option; draw a line 4 units long. You can increase or decrease it by 3 units. Issue the Lengthen command. All the options are displayed:

Select an object or [DElta/Percent/Total/DYnamic]:

If you select an object now, AutoCAD 2002 will simply tell you its length and then return you to the options again. You must select an option to change the object's length. Type DE for the Delta option. This will allow you to change the object's length by 3 units (-3 will decrease it, +3 will increase it). The prompt changes to:

Enter delta length or [Angle]<default>:   type in a length and
                                                press Enter

Select an object to change or [Undo]:

Note how two of the options begin with 'D' so you have to type the first two letters to distinguish them.

Be careful as to which part of the entity you select. Click near to the end you want the change to occur. Press Enter to finish the command.

Try each of the other options yourself.

Trim

How the command works

Trim allows you to clip off pieces of objects that intersect with other objects. Think of the Trim command as a pair of scissors which will cut along an edge (called a cutting edge). AutoCAD 2002 will ask you for a cutting edge. Once you tell it, it will want to know which objects you want to get rid of. Once you select these the command will trim them away.

Command line: trim, or the alias 'tr'

Menu: Modify>Trim

Toolbar:

If you select the wrong cutting edge just type 'u' and press Enter. AutoCAD 2002 will leave you in the command and you can proceed to selecting new objects.

The command in action

Issue the Trim command. Select the objects along which you want to cut or trim when you are asked:

Select cutting edges: This is actually one phrase. Read it as
Select objects: 'select the objects you want to form the
                                      cutting edge'

Press Enter to finish selecting the cutting edge. AutoCAD then responds with:

Select objects to trim or [Project/Edge/Undo]:

Press Enter to finish the command.

Trim will allow you to select several cutting edges at the same time.

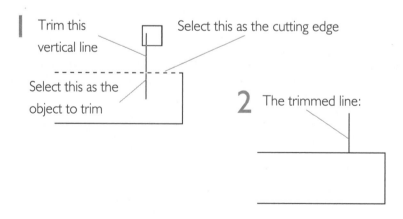

Trim this vertical line

Select this as the cutting edge

Select this as the object to trim

2 The trimmed line:

Extend

How the command works
You can extend the length of an object to meet another object. The object you are extending to is called the boundary. You cannot extend objects which are parallel because they will never meet.

Command line: extend, or the alias 'ex'

Menu: Modify>Extend

Toolbar:

The command in action
Issue the Extend command. Select the boundary you want to extend to in the usual way when AutoCAD 2002 prompts:

Select boundary edges: This is actually one phrase. Read it as
Select objects: 'select the objects you want to
                                       form the boundary edge'

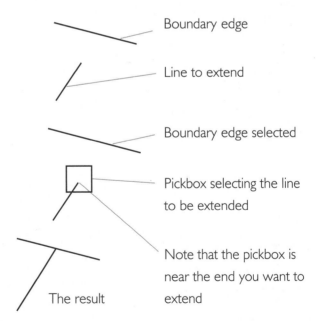

Boundary edge

Line to extend

Boundary edge selected

Pickbox selecting the line to be extended

Note that the pickbox is near the end you want to extend

The result

When AutoCAD 2002 asks you to select the object to extend, you must click on the side of the object near the boundary, otherwise AutoCAD 2002 will tell you there is no boundary in the other direction.

Chamfer

How the command works

Chamfer will join two lines by adding a third line. The easiest way to understand the command is to apply it to two lines joining at a right angle. AutoCAD 2002 will need to know how much of each line is to be removed (called the chamfer distance) before the third line is drawn to join the ends.

Command line: chamfer, or the alias 'cha'

Menu: Modify>Chamfer

Toolbar:

The command in action

Issue the Chamfer command. The current settings are displayed and the following options are displayed:

Select first line or [Polyline/Distance/Angle/Trim/Method]:

Before you select the line check the distance by typing 'd'.

1 You must input two chamfer distances. The first one applies to the first line you pick.

2 In both these cases the chamfer distance 1 was 30 units and the second distance was 10 units.

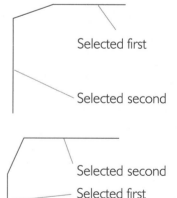

Selected first

Selected second

Selected second

Selected first

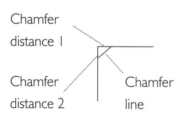

Chamfer distance 1

Chamfer distance 2

Chamfer line

Working with Layers

In this chapter you will learn to use layers. Layers are used to control the display of objects; they also help directly in the drawing and editing procedures by enabling you to assign colours and linetypes to them.

Covers

Chapter Nine

Layers

Introduction

An AutoCAD 2002 drawing can be constructed over several layers. A layer is like a transparent sheet of paper which holds drawing objects. For example, a drawing of the plans of a house could be constructed as follows: the walls would occupy a layer called 'walls', the doors and windows would be placed on a layer called 'fittings', etc. When a drawing is structured in this way you have control over numerous aspects of the work.

A layer can be assigned a linetype and a colour.

AutoCAD 2002 supplies you with one default layer named 0. Any other layers must be created by the you, the user, although you can assign as many layers as you like to a drawing. A layer is not limited in the number of objects it can hold. Each layer must have its own distinct name.

Layers always lie directly under each other and cannot be moved. Layers can be made visible or invisible, and can be assigned a colour or a linetype so that each object drawn on the layer will be in the specified colour and linetype.

Often the colour of a linetype is used to indicate the thickness of a line. Even if the printer/plotter device you use is monochrome, assigning colours to layers can be very important.

If you draw something on the wrong layer, AutoCAD 2002 will allow you to place it back on the correct layer.

This drawing is spread over four layers

Main structure of the drawing on this layer

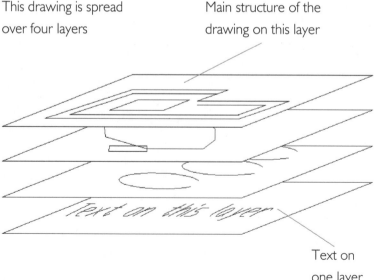

Text on one layer

Setting up a New Layer

Give layers names that describe what they contain.

Here we will set up two layers called Walls and Fittings. To create a new layer, first issue the Layer command:

Command line: layer, or the alias 'la'
Menu: Format>Layer...
Icon:

Controls which layers are displayed in the list here

In the Layer Properties Manager dialogue box, click on New.

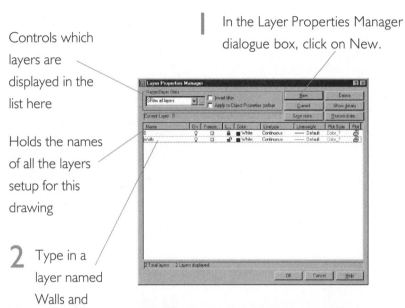

There is a special relationship between blocks and layers.

Holds the names of all the layers setup for this drawing

2 Type in a layer named Walls and press Enter.

You can rename a layer by highlighting its name and pressing the F2 function key.

The Walls layer is now in place. Click on 'Show details' to see its properties

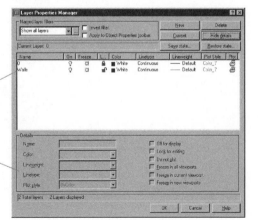

3 Try creating a new layer called Fittings

Assigning a Colour to a Layer

Assigning a colour to a layer means that everything drawn on that layer will take on that colour.

To assign the same colour to several layers at once, just hold the Ctrl key and click on the name of each layer. They will all be highlighted. Then click on the colour. This action opens the Select Color dialogue box.

1 Click on the colour box in the Color column.

2 Click on the colour red for the Walls layer in the Select Color dialogue box. Click OK.

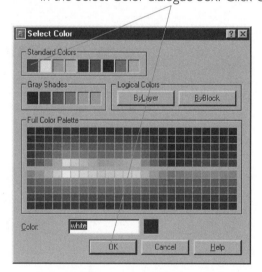

3 Assign the colour green to the layer Fittings.

Making a Layer Current

To follow these examples set up two layers: a 'Walls' layer with the colour red and a 'Fittings' layer in green.

A layer must be current before you can draw on it. To make the layer 'Walls' current, carry out the following easy steps:

1 Click on the layer name in the Layer Properties Manager dialogue box, then click on the Current button.

2 Click OK to return to the Drawing Editor.

3 The Object Properties toolbar at the top of the screen (see below) will show the name of the current layer and its colour. Try drawing something. It will appear in red.

Layers icon   Current layer and colour

Alternatively, to make a layer current from within the Drawing Editor:

1 Click here.

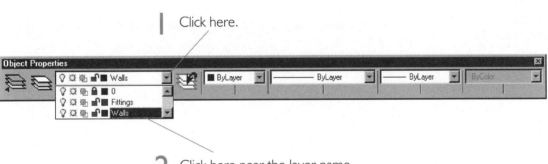

2 Click here near the layer name.

3 Click out on the Drawing Editor anywhere.

Draw an object such as a line or circle and it will take on the colour property of the layer selected.

Now make the 'Fittings' layer current and draw an object on it. It should appear in green.

Making Layers Visible or Invisible

Why control the visibility of layers?

AutoCAD 2002 allows you to switch a layer 'off' (invisible) or 'on' (visible).

A layer which is invisible is not printed. Sensitive information on a drawing can be placed on a separate layer and made invisible.

Complex drawings may become cluttered, which can make it difficult to select objects for editing or drawing. This clutter may be reduced by making a layer invisible if you are not working on it. When a layer is made invisible, the objects drawn on it disappear from the screen, but they still exist and are part of the drawing. Layers which are invisible are not printed. This has the advantage of allowing you to print selected layers of a drawing.

For example, a builder of a house may not be interested in the furnishings which an interior designer has placed on the drawing. The furnishings layer can be made invisible and the drawing then plotted for the builder.

Several layers can be made invisible if required. The icon for visible is a glowing light bulb. Invisibility is shown by a dull light bulb. To make a layer visible or invisible:

A yellow light bulb means the layer is on or visible.

1 Click here.

2 Click here on the light bulb.

3 Click out on the Drawing Editor anywhere.

It is advisable not to switch off the current layer.

Generally, there is no sense in making the layer you are working on (the current layer) invisible. If you attempt to switch it off, AutoCAD 2002 will warn you.

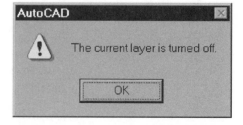

Linetypes

Introduction

The default linetype in AutoCAD 2002 is continuous. Everything you draw is shown with a continuous linetype. To draw with a dashed or dotted (or other) linetype you need to look in the two libraries of linetypes supplied. The libraries are found in the files *acadiso.lin* and *acltiso.lin*.

If the template drawing you use is based on the acltiso template, you should use the acltiso.lin library – see overleaf.

How to access a linetype

The steps for using a linetype are: firstly the linetype must be loaded into AutoCAD 2002 from a library, and secondly it must be set to 'current' status.

How to use a linetype

Once a linetype is loaded into AutoCAD 2002 you are ready to use it by making it current. That can be done in one of the following ways:

- Assign it to a layer – this is called the Bylayer method

- Assign it to a block – this is called the Byblock method

- Assign it to an object – to do this you just make the linetype current and draw

If you know how to set up your own template drawings, then load all the linetypes you frequently use into the template so that they are easily available.

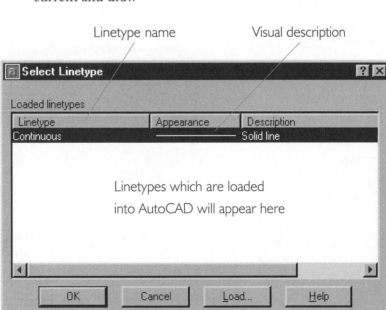

Linetype name   Visual description

How to Load a Linetype

1 In the Object Properties toolbar click on the linetype control down arrow or type Linetype at the command line.

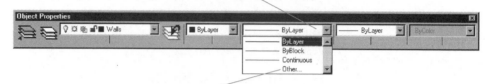

2 Click on Other. The Linetype Manager is displayed.

A linetype has to be loaded before it can be used.

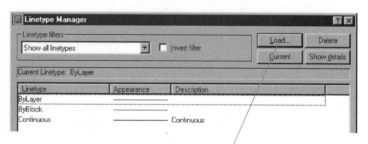

3 Click on Load

You can create your own linetype if there are none that suit you in the aclt or acltiso libraries.

4 Make sure acadiso.lin is in this box (see page 103).   If it's not then click on File... and select it from the library list.

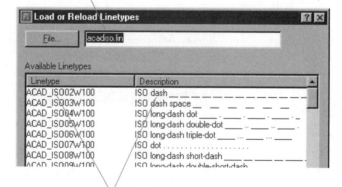

A linetype only has to be loaded once during the time you work on a file. It is saved with the file and is available the next time you open the drawing.

5 Click on the linetype you want to load – try ISO dash, and click OK.

6 The linetype is now loaded and added to the list in the Linetype Manager dialogue box. You may use the linetype in your drawing now. See the facing page.

Linetypes – ByLayer

Linetypes and layers – ByLayer

You can associate a linetype with a layer so that the linetype automatically becomes current when the layer is current. To do this follow these steps:

If the 'ltscale' setting is not correct, the linetype may still look continuous.

1 Open the Layer Properties Manager dialogue box by clicking on the icon 🗐 or Format>Layer.

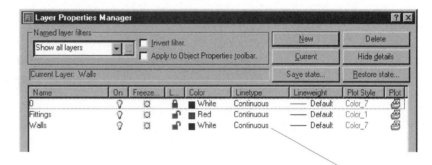

There are several other ways to carry out the procedures here. You may discover a more suitable way.

2 In the Layer Properties Manager dialogue box click on Continuous under Linetype.

3 The Select Linetype dialogue box opens. Select the linetype you want and click on OK. If it is not listed, click on Load and follow the procedure for loading a linetype.

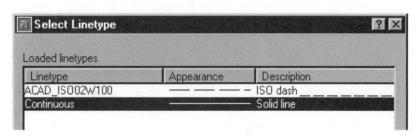

4 To see how successful you were, make the layer current and draw a line or two on it.

Linetypes by Object

Setting a linetype current

It is possible to draw different objects on the same layer with different linetypes. Simply draw the objects and use the grips to apply the loaded linetypes to them.

1 Pick on the object whose linetype you want to change. It will then display the grips.

2 In the Object Properties toolbar click on the linetype control down arrow.

3 Highlight the linetype you want to use. All the loaded linetypes will be displayed here.

AutoCAD 2002 allows you to assign a thickness to any linetype. For plotting purposes you can use the colour option by assigning a colour to a pen of a particular width.

4 Press the Esc key twice. This removes the grips from the selected object and applies the selected linetype.

Using the Modify Properties

The loaded linetypes are also available in the Properties dialogue box.

1 Pick on the object whose linetype you want to change. It will then display the grips.

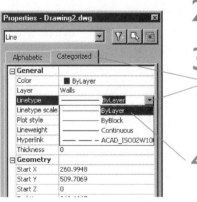

2 Go to Modify>Properties.

3 Click on the Categorized tab. The Linetype will be listed near the top. Click on it and click on the down arrow beside it.

4 Select the linetype you want.

Moving Objects to Different Layers

If you draw objects on the wrong layer, AutoCAD 2002 allows you to place them on the correct layer without redrawing them. Each object in a drawing has properties associated with it. The colour of an object or the layer it is on are examples of properties.

To change the layer an object is on you use the Change Properties command.

How the command works
Select the object you want to move to a new layer and then select the layer:

Command line: ddmodify

Menu: Modify>Properties...

If you have experience with AutoCAD 14 or any version of AutoCAD LT try using the ddchprop command.

The command in action

1 Issue the command and select the object(s) you want to move to a different layer.

2 Click on the Categorized tab. The Layer will be listed near the top. Click on it and click on the down arrow beside it.

3 The selected object will move to the chosen layer.

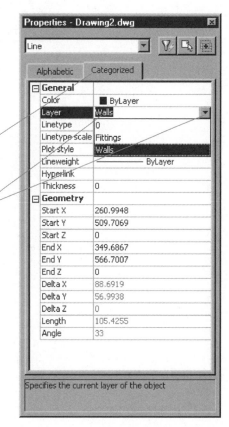

Scaling Linetypes – Ltscale

The examples here use the line object, but the same explanation applies for any object drawn in a particular linetype.

The scale of a linetype (or ltscale) refers to the spacing of its constituent elements. For example, the dashes in a linetype may be 4 units long and the spaces 2 units. These spacings can be scaled up or down from the defaults. The default setting is a scale of 1. To change the ltscale on a dashed linetype carry out the following:

1 From the Format menu select Linetype...

2 The Linetype Manager dialogue box is displayed.

3 Click on the linetype you want to readjust.

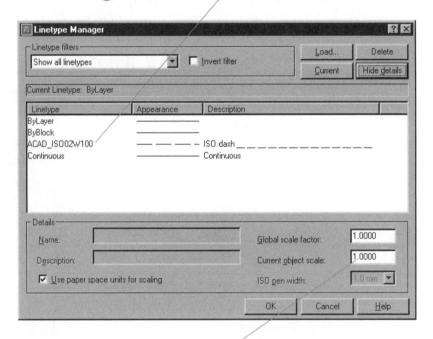

4 Enter the scale you want in Current object scale.

5 Click OK and draw a line. The new scale setting will apply.

To change the linetype scale of a line already drawn, you must use the Modify>Properties menu. Once the line is selected you can change its scale under the Categorized tab.

Blocks and Xrefs

Blocks are formed by grouping objects together. You will learn to insert blocks and drawings into other drawings. The difference between blocks and xrefs is explained, then an outline treatment of xrefs is covered.

Covers

Chapter Ten

What is a Block?

Once a block is made, you need a special procedure to edit it. See the Explode command on page 115.

A block is an object or group of objects which are gathered together and given a name. Once the group of objects has a name you can use it in the drawing as many times as you like. You can also use it in drawings other than the one it was created in.

You can build up your own library of blocks or purchase third party libraries. Typical examples of blocks are doors and windows, or electrical components such as switches and transistors.

A complete drawing can be treated as a block. For example you could draw a room and later add it into a separate drawing of a house.

A block has an insertion point. This is the point that it is picked up at for insertion into a drawing.

Three examples of blocks

Blocks should be drawn at real world size.

1. A block of a door:

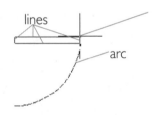

lines

Possible insertion point

arc

The arc and lines are grouped together and given a name. This is called a block

2. A block of a man:

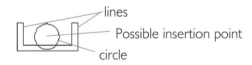

lines

Possible insertion point

circle

Keep all the blocks you make in a separate folder from the drawings.

3. A block of a barge:

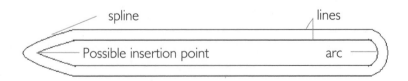

spline

lines

Possible insertion point

arc

Blocks and Layers

A block can be created on a single layer or spread over several layers. The layers a block is created on can affect the performance of the block when it's used in a drawing at a later stage.

Layer 0 blocks

Layer 0 is quite special. Any block created on layer 0 will position itself on the current layer when it is placed in a drawing. The block will then take on the properties of that layer.

If a block is spread over several layers, it will bring those layers into a drawing when it is inserted.

Here is an example. Imagine a drawing with just two layers: layer 0 (white) and layer Walls (red). If a block is created wholly on layer 0 it will be white in colour. If the user then makes layer Walls (red) current and proceeds to insert the block into the drawing, the block will sit into the layer Walls and appear red in colour.

Lastly, when this block is exploded for editing, it will fall back down to layer 0 and take on the properties of that layer.

Blocks created on layers other than 0

If a block is created on several layers other than layer 0, it will carry those layers and their properties around with it into whatever drawing it is inserted.

Layer 0 blocks have the special property of always inserting onto the current layer when placed into a drawing.

Here is an example. Imagine a block is created from objects on two layers: Walls (red) and Windows (yellow). If this block is inserted into a drawing that does not contain those layers, then the layers will be automatically created by the block as it is inserted. The layers will have the same properties as the original two layers – red and yellow. This will occur even if the current layer at the time of insertion is layer 0.

If this block is exploded for editing, the objects of the block will fall back to their original layers.

How to Make a Block

Overall view

- Draw the objects that make up the block.

- Give a name to the block.

- Decide on where the insertion point should be. This is important because you can insert the block into a drawing using Object Snap.

- Group the objects together.

Procedure

The example block being created here can only be inserted into the drawing it was created in.

1 Draw the door.

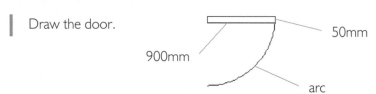

2 Click on Draw.

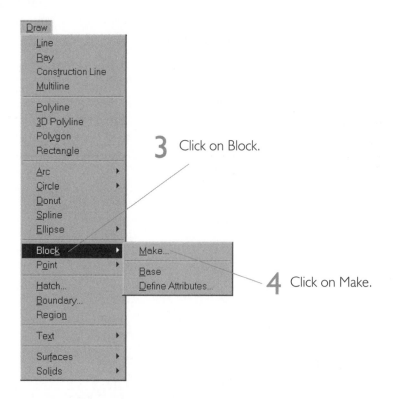

3 Click on Block.

4 Click on Make.

6 Click on Select objects. AutoCAD hides the dialogue box. Pull a selection window around the door and press Enter. This dialogue box will return.

5 Type 'Door1' in this area.

7 Click here and pick an insertion point – use Object Snap if you can.

8 Select here.

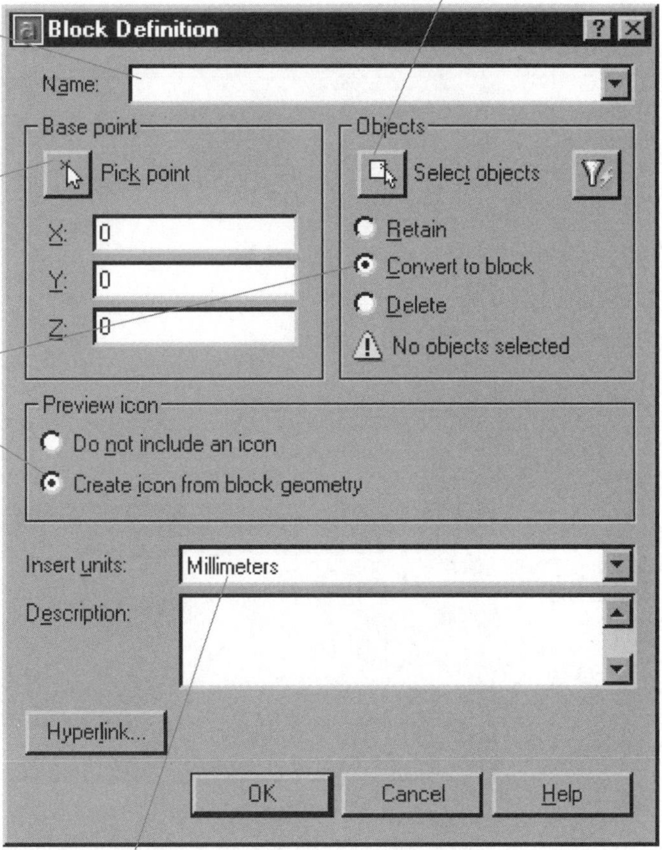

Block Definition ? ✕

Name: ▼

Base point
Pick point

X: 0
Y: 0
Z: 0

Objects
Select objects

○ Retain
● Convert to block
○ Delete
⚠ No objects selected

Preview icon
○ Do not include an icon
● Create icon from block geometry

Insert units: Millimeters ▼
Description:

Hyperlink...

OK   Cancel   Help

9 Units offered here are the drawing units.

10 Click on OK. AutoCAD 2002 creates the block.

How to Insert a Block

This block can only be inserted into the drawing it was created in.

Once the block has been created, you may insert it into the drawing. Try this now using the block 'Door1':

I   Click on the Insert menu.

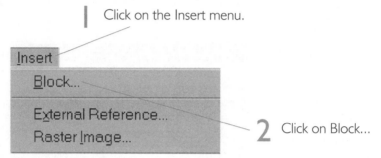

2   Click on Block...

3   The Insert dialogue box will appear.

4   Click on the down arrow. All the blocks created in the current drawing will be listed. Select the block name.

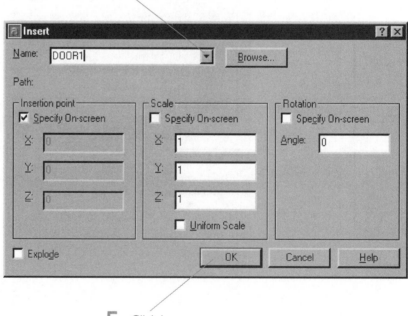

5   Click here.

There is a close relationship between blocks and layers. Make sure you understand layers before you create a library of blocks.

6 At this point you are returned to the drawing with the block attached to the cross-hairs at the insertion point you defined.

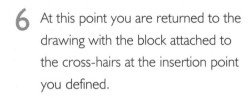

7 Move the block into position on the screen. The command line asks for the Insertion point and lists several options:

[Scale/X/Y/Z/Rotate/PScale/PX/PY/PZ/PRotate]:

These options refer to the scaling and rotation of the block. If you simply pick a point on the screen the block will be inserted without being scaled (at the size it was drawn).

8 The block is now locked into position in the drawing.

This block will behave as one object when you try to edit it. Try the Move command on it, for example. The moment you select it, it will appear as a single entity.

Exploding a block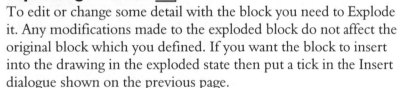

To edit or change some detail with the block you need to Explode it. Any modifications made to the exploded block do not affect the original block which you defined. If you want the block to insert into the drawing in the exploded state then put a tick in the Insert dialogue shown on the previous page.

Any drawing can be inserted into any other drawing.

If you don't have the time to master layers before working on blocks, just make sure that you use the default layer 0 when creating the blocks.

How to Use a Block in any Drawing

If a block is converted into a drawing file then you can use it in any other drawing created by AutoCAD 2002.

1   Type 'wblock' at the command line and press Enter.

2   The Write Block dialogue box appears.

A block does not exist as a file on the hard disk until you wblock it.

3   Select Block.

4   Click on the down arrow and select the block name.

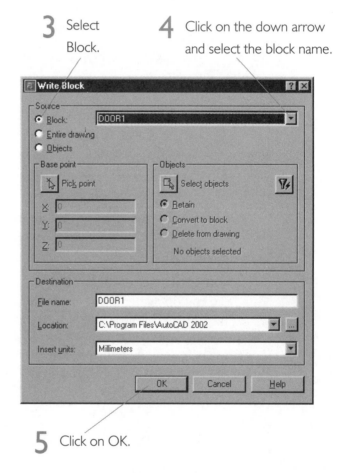

5   Click on OK.

At this stage AutoCAD 2002 takes the block and converts it to a drawing (in this case DOOR1). This drawing DOOR1 can be treated like any AutoCAD drawing. You can, for example, open it as a separate drawing, explode it, edit and draw in the usual way.

External References – Xrefs

External references (or xrefs) allow you to link two or more drawings together. Below are three separate drawings:

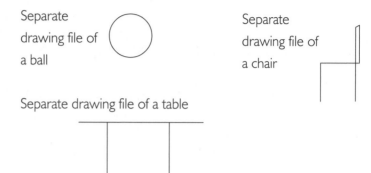

Separate drawing file of a ball

Separate drawing file of a chair

Separate drawing file of a table

The drawing of the table could make reference to the ball and chair drawings to produce the following drawing.

In this case the table is the *master* drawing which has made reference to two external drawings – the chair and the ball. The ball and chair drawings are not inserted into the master drawing of the table (as a block could be), but instead are *attached* to the table drawing.

The Xref command will allow you to attach drawings to a master drawing.

If the drawing file of the chair is changed in any way, then the chair in the master drawing will change also. This is better than if the chair was inserted as a block, because if the block drawing was changed, then the change would not be seen in the master drawing.

A block becomes part of the drawing it was inserted into: an external reference always remains a separate drawing.

How to Use Xrefs

To follow this section on xrefs you should create three simple drawings – of the chair, table and ball – and name them accordingly. The ball is a simple circle while the table and chair are constructed from lines. Create each of the images on a sheet of 420mm by 297 mm. Once you have done this open the drawing of the table. You will then attach the drawing of the ball by making an xref to it.

Attaching the Xref files – ball and chair

Issue the Xref command by either typing xref at the command line and pressing Enter or from the Insert toolbar select [icon]. The drop-down menu option is shown here:

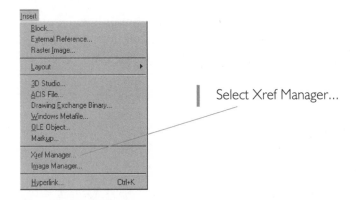

Select Xref Manager...

2 Click on Attach to proceed.

3 From the Select Reference File dialogue box, highlight the file you want. Then click Open.

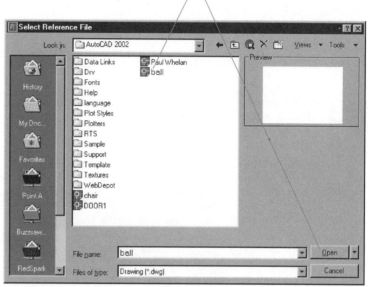

4 The External Reference dialogue box will confirm the selection. Click OK to continue.

Make sure the dot is in here

You may scale the drawing. In this example leave it unscaled (that is 1)

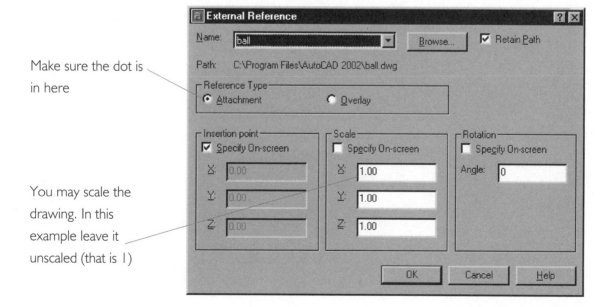

...cont'd

5 The drawing will appear attached to the crosshairs. Position it on the table.

6 Issue the Xref Manager command again.

An xref file is not part of the drawing it is attached to: it is referenced.

7 Click on Attach in the dialogue box.

8 Click on Browse.

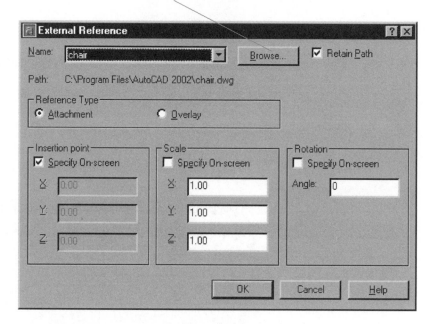

9 Select the Chair file and click on Open, and then on OK and position the chair in the drawing.

10 The files are attached. Save the drawing.

The Value of Xrefs

An xref will update automatically in the drawing it is attached to.

The value of xrefs will now be illustrated.

1 Open the drawing of the chair and edit it so that is looks like this:

2 Now save the chair and open the drawing of the ball. Edit it to look like this:

3 Save the ball drawing and open the table drawing. It should look like this:

A block becomes part of the drawing it is inserted into. Blocks will not update when they are modified.

A drawing can have any number of xrefs.

The edits to the attached drawing are reflected in the master drawing. This occurs because the xrefs are not saved with the drawing table. Only the link to the attachments is saved. Each time the master drawing table is open it checks what is in the attached drawing: any changes made to them are automatically displayed.

The value of this can be seen on large projects. A master drawing can contain references to other drawings. Each of the attached drawings can be as complex as you like and can be created by different individuals on a network. As work proceeds, the master drawing will always show the latest state of the drawings.

Working with Xrefs

A drawing which has an external reference must always have access to the referenced drawing while it is attached. This means that you cannot move the master drawing or the xrefs to another folder. The illustration below shows four folders: folder 1 contains the master drawing with xrefs in folders 2, 3 and 4. If the xref in folder 2 is moved to folder 3, then the master drawing will not be able to find it.

Try and keep the master drawing and its xrefs in the same folder.

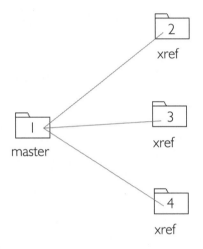

A master drawing will always look for its external references each time the drawing is opened.

This can lead to problems if a large number of xrefs are being used. A good tip for this kind of work is to keep the master drawing and all its external references in one folder. It is then easy to move the master drawing and its xrefs, particularly if you want to send the drawing to someone else to complete.

When a project is finished you can bind the xrefs into the master drawing so that they behave like blocks: they become part of the drawing and do not update automatically. The master drawing will not look for them again.

Do not move the location of an xref. If you do, the master drawing will not be able to find it.

Dimensioning

The primary function of a Computer Aided Design drawing is to supply enough information about an object to enable its construction. Dimensioning is an essential visual guide to helping someone to interpret the drawing for construction. AutoCAD 2002 has many tools for dimensioning drawings, positioning the dimensions and later editing them. In this chapter you will be introduced to many of these dimensioning tools and the techniques for using them.

Covers

Chapter Eleven

Dimensioning

AutoCAD 2002 has many tools to help you to place dimensions on a drawing. There is no need to draw dimension lines or calculate a dimension value. AutoCAD 2002 will do this for you. Some of the terms used in conjunction with dimensioning are illustrated below:

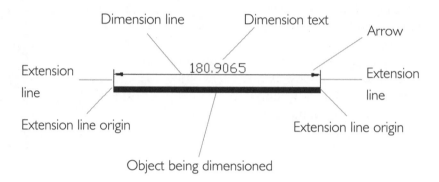

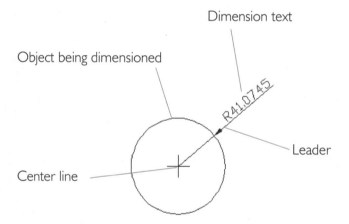

Associative dimensioning

The term associative dimensioning means that the dimension is associated with an object. When the object being dimensioned is changed, that change is shown immediately in the dimension. There is no need to re-dimension the object. Associative dimensioning can be switched off.

The Dimensioning Toolbar

To call up the dimensioning toolbar use the View drop down menu: View>Toolbars, and place an x opposite Dimension in the list of toolbars.

Dimension Style: enables the creation of styles for dimensioning in engineering or architectural drawing, etc.

The name of the current Dimension Style

Dimension Update: allows a dimension style to be updated

Dimension Text Edit: enables the editing of the dimension text

Dimension Edit: allows you to reposition the dimension text

Center Mark: places center marks on circles and arcs

Tolerance: allows the insertion of geometric tolerances

Quick Leader Line: used for annotations

Continue dimension: allows contiguous dimensions to be aligned

Baseline Dimension: allows dimensions from a datum line

Quick Dimension

Angular Dimension: dimension angles

Diameter Dimension: places a diameter dimension on circles

Radius Dimension: places a radius dimension on circles and arcs

Ordinate Dimensions: also called datum dimensions that measure a perpendicular distance from an origin. The origin can be specified by the user

Aligned Dimension: dimensions lines which are not horizontal or vertical

Linear Dimension: dimensions horizontal and vertical lines

Linear Dimensioning

To dimension an object (it can be horizontal or vertical) follow the steps below. In this example the dimension is applied to a horizontal polyline.

1 Click on the Linear dimension icon. AutoCAD 2002 responds with 'Specify first extension line origin or select object'.

2 Press the Enter key or the right mouse button and AutoCAD responds 'Select object to dimension'.

3 Select the polyline by clicking on it. AutoCAD 2002 immediately calculates the length of the object and now asks:

'Dimension line location?' or [Mtext/Text/Angle/Horizontal/Vertical/Rotated]:

Read the command line carefully throughout the dimensioning procedures.

4 To position the dimension line move the cursor above or below the polyline and pick a point. The dimension is now locked into position.

Unhappy with how the dimension looks?

The dimension text may look too small or too big; the arrows may be the wrong size, or perhaps the extension lines run too close to the polyline. All these features can be individually modified to form a dimensioning style. For the moment we will change all the above elements by scaling them up. The setting for the size of all the dimension elements is held in a system variable (see page 40) called DIMSCALE. By changing the dimscale value you affect the display of the dimension. Try the following:

1 Type DIMSCALE at the command line and press Enter. The response may be 'New value for DIMSCALE <1.0000>:'

2 Type in a value greater than the default value. Try 2 in this case and press Enter.

3 AutoCAD 2002 returns you to a blank line prompt. Nothing appears to have happened. You now need to update the dimension to see the effect of the new setting. Click on the Dimension Update icon .

4 Select the dimension. Selection is made by clicking anywhere on the dimension (text or lines). The dimension will highlight. Press Enter.

5 All aspects of the dimension will increase in size; the arrows, the text, etc.

The dimensioned polyline when DIMSCALE was set to 1

The dimensioned polyline is shown below when the Update Dimension was applied after the DIMSCALE value was set to 2.

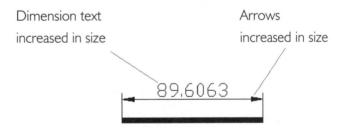

Dimension text increased in size

Arrows increased in size

Dimscale affects the setting in the leader lines. Dimscale does not affect the actual length of a dimension or the object being dimensioned.

Object Snap and Dimensioning

The Object Snap tools may be used to tell AutoCAD the position of the extension lines. This is useful if you are dimensioning across several different lines. Consider the case below where a line and a polyline run end to end. The linear dimension must measure from one end of the line to the other end of the polyline.

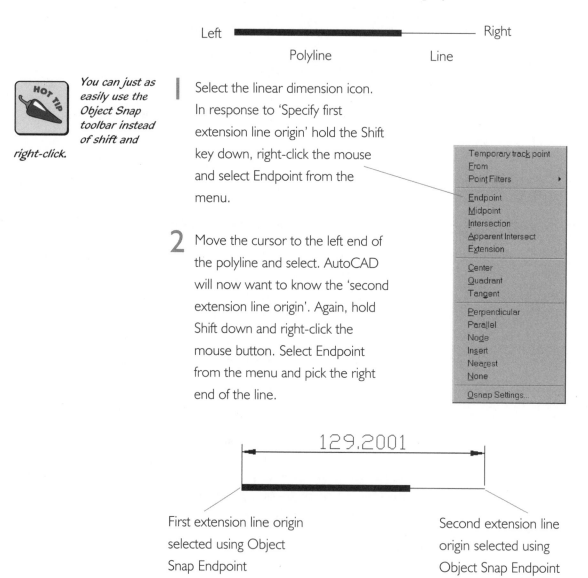

You can just as easily use the Object Snap toolbar instead of shift and right-click.

1 Select the linear dimension icon. In response to 'Specify first extension line origin' hold the Shift key down, right-click the mouse and select Endpoint from the menu.

2 Move the cursor to the left end of the polyline and select. AutoCAD will now want to know the 'second extension line origin'. Again, hold Shift down and right-click the mouse button. Select Endpoint from the menu and pick the right end of the line.

First extension line origin selected using Object Snap Endpoint

Second extension line origin selected using Object Snap Endpoint

Aligned Dimensioning

The aligned dimension is for linear objects which are not vertical or horizontal. However, it may also be used for horizontal and vertical lines. It works the same way as the linear dimensioning on page 126.

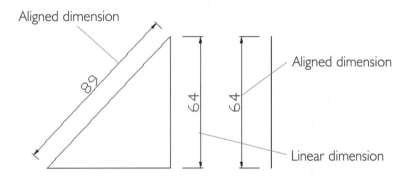

Aligned dimension

Aligned dimension

Linear dimension

In this illustration the vertical lines were dimensioned with the linear and aligned options.

Quick Dimension

The Quick Dimension icon allows you to easily dimension objects using the continued, ordinate or baseline options. When the command is issued AutoCAD will ask you to: 'Select geometry to dimension'. You can pick several objects and then press Enter to finish the selection. AutoCAD 2002 next offers you the options:

'Specify dimension line position, or [Continuous, Staggered/ Baseline/Ordinate/Radius/Diameter/datumPoint/ Edit],<Continuous>,'

If you pick a point to anchor the dimension line, AutoCAD will use the default 'continuous' option (defaults are in angled brackets>), otherwise select an option by typing the uppercase letter from the options.

Try drawing 3 or 4 continuous lines and dimension using the baseline option.

Radius and Diameter

AutoCAD 2002 can quickly calculate the radius and diameter of circles, arcs and fillet arcs. In the case of a radius it places the letter 'R' for radius in front of the measurement and for diameters it places the diameter symbol.

To position a radius, click on the radius icon and select the arc or circle. You can move the values into position by moving the cursor. Try placing them inside and outside a circle.

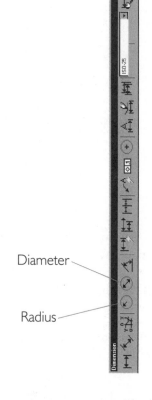

Diameter

Radius

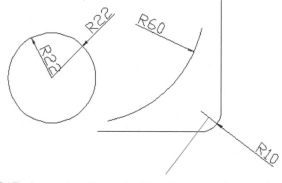

AutoCAD draws the dimension line from the centre of the selected arc or circle automatically

To position a diameter, click on the diameter icon and select the arc or circle. You can move the values into position by moving the cursor. Try placing them inside and outside a circle.

To lock the dimensioning into vertical and horizontal positions, switch to Ortho mode (the F8 function key) before you dimension.

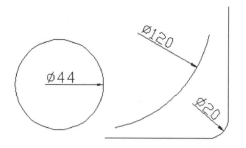

Continue Dimensioning

The Continue dimension allows you to run a series of linear dimensions which are always positioned at the same level. You can see an example in the illustration below. The first value of 33 was put into place using the Linear dimension option and the 45 value was input using the Continue option. AutoCAD automatically lined up the 45 value with the 33 value. This is what the Continue option does.

To try this, draw a shape similar to that shown below. Here are the steps involved:

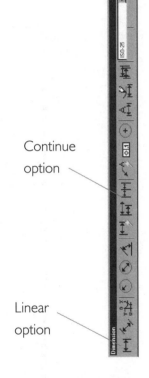

Continue option

Linear option

1 Place the 33 on the first line segment in the usual way using the Linear option (your value does not have to be 33).

2 Now select the Continue option. AutoCAD will ask for a 'Second extension line origin' (not a first!). Pick the end of the second line segment. The dimension line is aligned correctly. Press Enter twice to end the command.

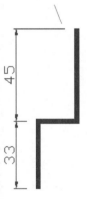

End of second line segment

Using Continue on existing dimensions

If you try to use Continue on a dimension you did some time ago (say during a previous drawing session) AutoCAD will ask you to pick the dimension you want to 'continue' from by prompting 'Select base dimension'. Pick the existing dimension and proceed as above when you see the prompt 'Second extension line origin'.

Position the first dimension with care as AutoCAD will align all the other dimensions with it.

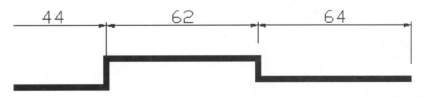

Continuous dimensioning

Baseline Dimensioning

Baseline dimensioning will refer all dimensions back to a datum line. The dimensions are stacked one above the other. The distance separating the dimensions is controlled by the system variable DIMDLI.

A datum line is a reference point.

To try this dimensioning, draw a vertical line with some smaller lines running off it. Here are the steps involved:

1 Place the 35 dimension value on the first segment using the Linear dimension option (your value does not have to be 35).

2 Click on the Baseline icon and respond to the prompt 'Specify a second extension line origin' by using Object Snap to pick at point B in the illustration.

3 The dimension line is positioned a preset distance (which can be changed) out from the first dimension line.

4 AutoCAD again asks for 'a second extension line origin'. Pick point C and press Enter twice to finish the command.

Baseline

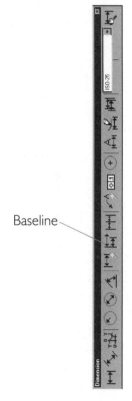

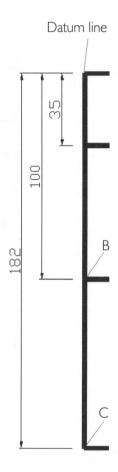

Datum line

Angular Dimensioning

As you move the cursor to position the dimension line, notice how AutoCAD will place the arrows outside the angle as you move toward the apex of the angle.

Acute and obtuse angles can be measured using the Angular dimensioning option. Draw some lines in the shape of 'z' to practise applying angular dimensions.

1 Click the Angular icon.

2 In response to 'Select arc, circle or line <specify vertex>', click on a line.

3 To the second response 'Select second line', select the second line. As you move the cursor you will see AutoCAD 2002 offering you various dimensioning formats. Try moving the cursor along the area within the acute angle and click when you like the format.

Try the same for the obtuse angle. All the angles below were placed by moving the cursor into different positions.

Angular

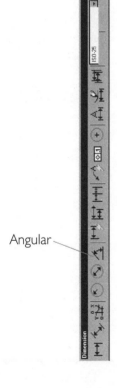

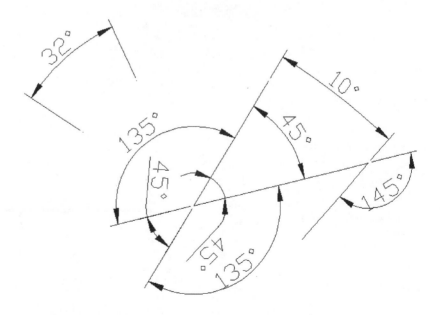

Editing a Dimension

Text that is part of a dimension cannot be edited with the normal text commands 'mtext' and 'dtext'. There are several ways to edit the dimension text:

Command line: 'dimtedit'

Menu: Dimension>Align Text

Use grips

Dimension>Align Text

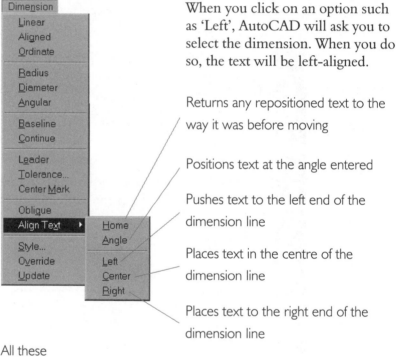

When you click on an option such as 'Left', AutoCAD will ask you to select the dimension. When you do so, the text will be left-aligned.

Returns any repositioned text to the way it was before moving

Positions text at the angle entered

Pushes text to the left end of the dimension line

Places text in the centre of the dimension line

Places text to the right end of the dimension line

If you are constantly editing dimensions you should consider setting up a dimensioning style.

All these dimensions were originally centred, but after editing some are left aligned and rotated at 45°

Typing 'dimtedit' at the command line (and pressing ENTER) offers the same options of Left, Right, Center, Home and Angle, however it also allows you to reposition the text using the cursor. Try executing the command now. AutoCAD 2002 will ask you to select the text for editing. The moment the dimension is selected the dimension text will move with the cursor. Simply pick a new location to reposition it. The extension lines will also follow the cursor movement so that you can lengthen or shorten them.

You can select several dimensions at once and apply the edit changes to all the dimensions.

This dimension had the text moved to a new position and the extension lines stretched. See the original dimension on the previous page

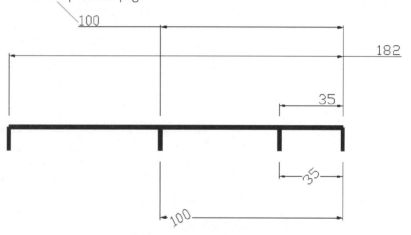

Using grips to edit a dimension

Click on the dimension when the command line is blank. The grips will appear. Notice the grip at the centre point of the text. This grip can be selected by clicking on it and the text then moved into position.

This grip can be used to move the text or stretch the extension lines

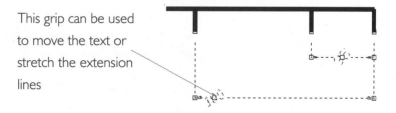

The DIMEDIT Command

Dimedit allows you to easily replace the dimension text itself. The command is typed at the command line. Each of the options is described here:

The extension lines may be controlled by setting up a dimension style.

Home	Returns the text to the position it had before it was moved.
Rotate	Rotates the dimension text.
Oblique	Repositions the extension lines at a new angle. The default position is at 90 degrees to the dimension line. An obliquing angle of 45 degrees is shown in the illustration below.
New	Allows you to replace the dimension text. Once the option New is selected, the multiline text editor is open. Just type the new text in the editor and click OK. The old text is represented by <>. To remove the old text you must remove these symbols in the multiline text editor.

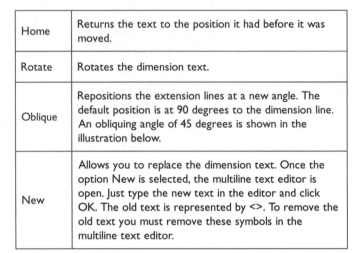

The new text

The extension lines were set to an angle of 45 degrees using the oblique option

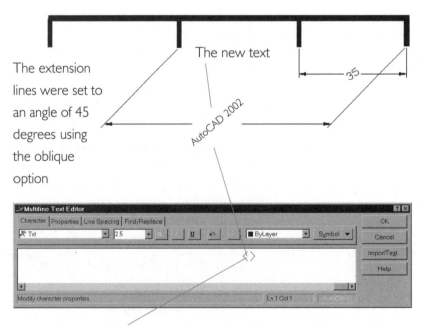

The markers '< >' symbolise the old text. If you leave these here the old text will remain

3D Drawing – an Introduction

In this chapter, you'll learn to define user coordinate planes for constructing a 3D drawing. It is essential to master this aspect of 3D drawing before you proceed any further.

Covers

Chapter Twelve

The Coordinate Plane

People are good at drawing and illustrating objects in 2D. All drawing in AutoCAD is carried out on the X–Y plane in 2D. To construct a 3D drawing in AutoCAD you simply move the X–Y plane around in space, building up the 3D model.

A simplified description of this technique applied to drawing a house in 3D is:

1 Draw the floor say as a rectangle.

The UCSICON command controls the visibility of the WCS or UCS icon.

2 Turn the X–Y plane up at 90 degrees and draw the walls.

3 Move the X–Y plane up, tilt it at 45 degrees and draw the sloping roof.

From this description you can see that you must be competent at moving the X–Y plane around in the space that the drawing will occupy. The World Coordinate System icon will help you to do this.

Visibility of the World Coordinate System icon

The icon is found at the bottom left of the screen. If it is not visible, you can switch it on using the command UCSICON. The options available are:

The World Coordinate System icon will not print with the drawing.

[ON/OFF All/Noorigin/ORigin/Properties]<ON>

ON will display the icon on the screen. Select 'P' for Properties. The following screen is displayed:

Select 2D to display a flat icon. This icon will be used for the rest of this chapter

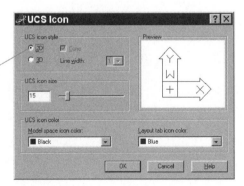

A Closer Look at the WCS Icon

When a new drawing is setup in AutoCAD 2002, you are presented with the World Coordinate System icon. This icon changes as you define new coordinate planes.

The icon is used to show you your orientation in a drawing.

Here the icon shows that it is the World Coordinate System and that the intersection of the X and Y axes is at the origin 0,0

The cross marks the origin of the plane

Z axis points up towards you

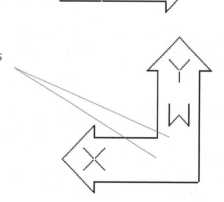

Y axis

W for World

X axis

It can sometimes be difficult to know whether you are under or over an object: the X and Y axes do not intersect when you are below an object.

Here the icon is again showing the World Coordinate System, but the missing cross shows that it is not sitting at the origin

The cross is missing

Y axis

W for World

X axis

Here the intersecting lines are missing. This means that you are below the plane looking up at the object (a worm's eye view)

The UCSICON Command

This command is responsible for the display of the UCS (User Coordinate System) icon. Its most valuable usage is to make the UCS icon follow you around as you define new coordinate systems. This way it will show you the orientation of the X and Y axes at all times.

The options within this invaluable command are explained. The icon can be switched on or off by selecting View>Display>UCS Icon>On or Origin.

On/Off selected by clicking here

The UCSICON command controls the visibility of the WCS or UCS icon.

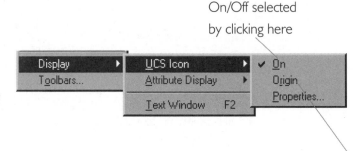

Forces the icon to follow, wherever you define the origin of the UCS

UCSICON at the command line options

The UCS icon does not print on a drawing.

ON	Makes the icon visible.
OFF	Makes the icon invisible.
All	Makes the icon visible in all the viewports.
Noorigin	Places the icon at the bottom left of the screen, regardless of the position of the icon on the screen.
Origin	Places the icon at the point at which you defined the origin (0,0). If the icon does not position itself over the origin when this option is on, you will need to zoom out from the drawing a little.
Properties	Allows the icon's properties to be modified – typically, its colour, size or style.

Other Orientations of the UCS

The previous illustrations of the UCS showed it when it was on the default World coordinate plane. If you define a new plane for drawing, the icon may take up the following positions:

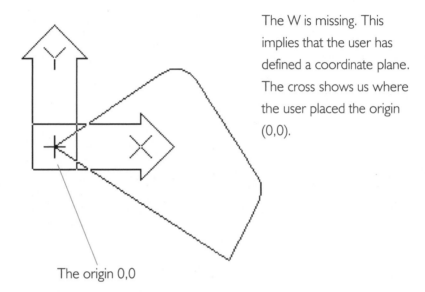

The W is missing. This implies that the user has defined a coordinate plane. The cross shows us where the user placed the origin (0,0).

The origin 0,0

The same object viewed from underneath:

The cross representing the origin may not appear if the icon is too near the edge of the screen. Try zooming out.

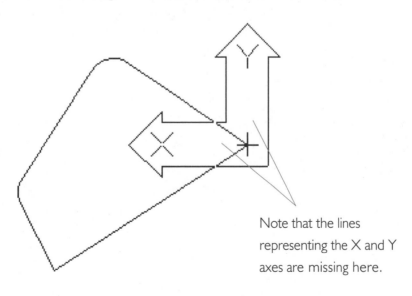

Note that the lines representing the X and Y axes are missing here.

Drawing your own Axes

To understand the UCS and UCSICON command you will need to follow the exercises over the next few pages.

Effectively, what you will do here is draw your own X, Y and Z axes and then learn to move the UCS around them.

1 Start a new drawing on an A3 sheet in decimal units. Leave the grid on.

2 Using polar coordinates, draw a line 100 units from the origin 0,0 to represent the X axis (@100<0).

3 Using polar coordinates draw a line 100 units from the origin 0,0 to represent the Y axis (@100<90).

4 Do not use polar coordinates to draw the Z axis. Instead, try the following: Start the line command in the usual way and in response to 'From point' type in 0,0. In response to 'To point' enter the absolute coordinate 0,0,100.

As you cannot see the Z axis it is better to change your view of the drawing. Using the command View>3D Views>Viewpoint Presets, set the view to 315 degrees from the X axis and 45 degrees from the XY plane.

 If you do not change your view then the Z axis points toward you out of the screen so you will not be able to see it until you change your viewpoint.

Your image should look like that on the right. The icon shows the orientation of the axes.

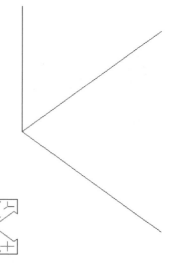

The X–Y Plane and the Origin

When you place text on this drawing of the axes, the plane that you are drawing on is clearly illustrated. Try the following: use the text command to place text of about 8 units high along the X axis (orientation 0 degrees) and along the Y axis (orientation 90 degrees). The drawing will now look similar to the illustration below.

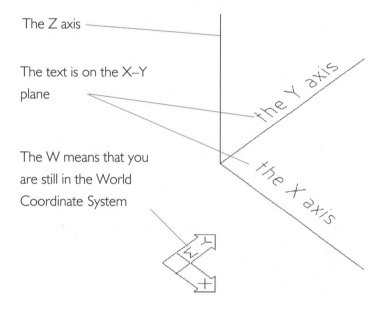

The Z axis

The text is on the X–Y plane

The W means that you are still in the World Coordinate System

Note the appearance of the cross when the icon moves to the origin.

Moving the icon to the origin

The origin is at the intersection of the three axes. To place the icon at this point carry out the following.

If the icon does not move to the origin, you may have the intersection of the axes too close to the edge of the screen.

1. Type UCSICON at the command line.

2. Type OR to select the option ORigin and press Enter. The icon should jump to the intersection of the axes.

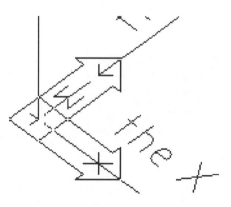

Moving the UCS up the Z axis

The X–Y drawing plane can be moved up the Z axis by moving the origin up the Z axis. The UCS icon will move up the axis to confirm this for you. Follow these steps:

1. Type UCS at the command line to define the new drawing plane and press Enter.

2. Type M for Move to tell AutoCAD that you wish to move the origin.

3. AutoCAD responds by telling you that the origin is at 0,0,0 and asks ' Specify new origin point or [Zdepth]<0,0,0>'.

4. Type MID to move the origin to the mid point of the Z axis. In response to 'OF', click on the Z axis.

AutoCAD's editing and drawing commands only work properly on the current UCS.

The icon will position itself half-way along the Z axis. Try drawing a circle on this new plane with its centre at 0,0 and a radius of 10 units.

The origin of the new UCS plane is now here

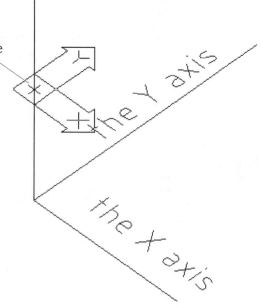

Don't forget to use the flat 2D icon as it's easier to visualise the plane you are working on. See page 138.

Naming a UCS

Give the UCS a name that will imply what it is used for.

As a drawing grows in complexity the need to return to a user-defined coordinate system becomes evident. AutoCAD allows you to do this by naming a UCS that you set up. For example, on the previous page the UCS was moved half way up a line representing the Z axis. This coordinate plane can be named as follows:

1 Type 'dducs' at the command line and press Enter or use the menus: Tools>Named UCS...

2 The current UCS is labelled UNNAMED. Name it by highlighting it and pressing the function key F2. Type in the new name.

3 Click OK.

A UCS may also be named by typing UCS at the command line. AutoCAD responds with the options:

[New/Move/orthoGraphic/Prev/Restore/Save/Del/Apply/?/ World]<World>:

Typing S will allow you to Save the current view. Typing R will allow you to Restore an already saved view.

Returning to the World System

Most drawings will start from the default World Coordinate System. Consequently, it is important that you can return there easily.

1 Type 'dducs' at the command line and press Enter or use the menus: Tools>Named UCS...

2 Click on World.

If you lose your orientation in a drawing, name the UCS you are on and return to the World Coordinate System.

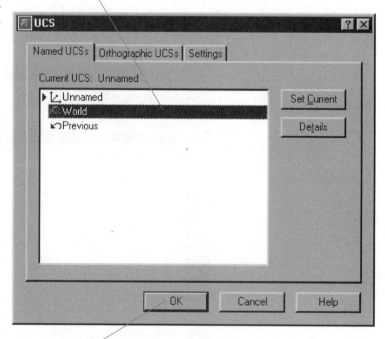

The World Coordinate System is the default system which AutoCAD offers.

3 Click OK. The World Coordinate System becomes current.

Notice how the icon drops back to its original position. Any editing or drawing carried out now will be on the original X–Y plane.

Returning to a Named UCS

Any UCS which has a name attached can be called back to the screen very quickly. This prevents having to redefine a UCS each time you want to return to it. To restore the UCS named 'Half way up the Z axis', carry out the following steps:

You can also restore a UCS at the command line by typing 'UCS' and 'r' for restore.

1 Type 'dducs' at the command line and press Enter or use the menus: Tools>Named UCS...

2 Click on 'Half way up the Z axis'.

3 Click OK.

A UCS may also be restored by typing UCS at the command line. AutoCAD responds with the options:

A 'UCS' name can be up to 31 characters long. All UCS names are converted to upper case letters.

[New/Move/orthoGraphic/Prev/Restore/Save/Del/Apply/?/World]<World>:

Typing R will allow you to Restore an already saved view. If you cannot remember its name (or how you spelled it) enter the '?' mark and press Enter twice. A text box will open with the names listed. Enter the name you want. You may need to close the text box in the standard Windows manner.

Rotating the UCS around the X Axis

AutoCAD allows you to set up a new UCS by rotating the coordinate plane you are working on around the X axis. Before you try doing this, make sure you are back at the World Coordinate System in the drawing of the axes created on page 142, or in a situation similar to that shown below:

If you are doing this exercise on a new drawing in the World Coordinate System then make sure that you view it from 315 degrees in the X axis and 45 degrees in the XY plane (for how to do this, refer back to the Viewpoint Presets dialogue on page 73).

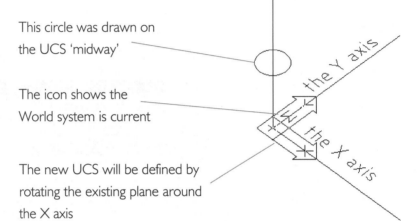

This circle was drawn on the UCS 'midway'

The icon shows the World system is current

The new UCS will be defined by rotating the existing plane around the X axis

Issue the command UCS at the command prompt and press Enter. Type N to select the option New. Type X to rotate around the X axis and press Enter. AutoCAD will ask you for an angle of rotation. Type 90 (degrees) and press Enter.

The drop-down menu option is Tools>New UCS>X. Look at the command line and enter 90 degrees.

The icon will rotate into the position shown in this illustration. Try entering some text to see how it will align. Finish by naming the new UCS as 'upright'

The text aligns itself along the new plane you have defined

Rotating the UCS around the Y Axis

If you succeeded in setting up the UCS on the previous page, the Y axis now has a different orientation than when it was in the World Coordinate System. You will now set up a new UCS by rotating around the Y axis by 90 degrees.

Notice how the crosshairs always align to the X and Y axes.

This circle was drawn on the UCS 'midway'

The new UCS will be defined by rotating the existing plane around the Y axis

The cross shows where the origin is

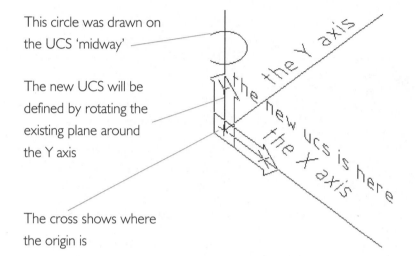

Issue the command UCS at the command prompt and press Enter. Type N to select the option New. Type Y to rotate around the Y axis and press Enter. AutoCAD will ask you for an angle of rotation. Type 90 (degrees) and press Enter.

Any time you set up a new UCS, try putting some text on it. It's the best way to understand if the orientation is as you wanted it to be.

The text aligns itself along the new plane you have defined

The icon will rotate into the position shown in this illustration. Try entering some text to see how it will align. Finish by naming the new UCS as 'backplane'

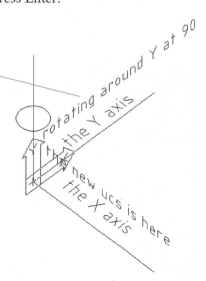

Looking at a UCS from Behind

With all the user defined planes you have set up so far, the view was from the front (like looking in a mirror). To see what happens if you define a UCS so that you are looking at it from behind (like being inside the mirror, looking out), try the following using the UCS 'backplane' which you set up on the previous page.

Issue the UCS command. Type N to select the option New. Type Y and press Enter. Type in 180 (degrees) to rotate the plane (anticlockwise if you refer to the circle in the drawing). There are several features worth noting:

Editing and drawing from behind a plane can be difficult, especially if you're inputting distance values such as in polar coordinates.

1. The crossing lines on the icon are missing. This means that you are behind the plane.

2. Any text you type will be viewed from behind (like looking out from behind a mirror at something written on the mirror).

3. The positive side of the X axis is now running to the left.

The situation is illustrated below:

The drawing can be viewed from any position using the View command.

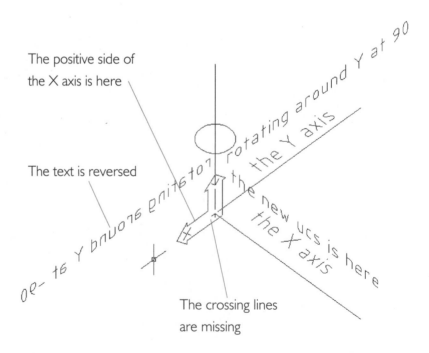

The positive side of the X axis is here

The text is reversed

The crossing lines are missing

Using the Viewports

The use of viewports is essential in 3D drawing. Refer to pages 66–68 for instructions on setting up viewports. Viewports give you different views of the same drawing. The editing and drawing you carry out in one viewport is reflected in the other. This allows you to judge immediately whether your actions make sense in 3D space or not. To illustrate this, set up two horizontal viewports of the drawing.

The two viewports show the same view initially. Now change the view in the bottom viewport by using the drop down menu View>3D Views>Viewport Presets. Use the following values: 225 from the X axis and 45 from the XY plane. Note the changes in the view labelled below:

You may need to change the zoom magnification to set the drawing up to imitate these views.

1 The text you previously saw face-on is now viewed from behind.

2 The cross lines are visible where the axes intersect, indicating that you are viewing the plane from the front.

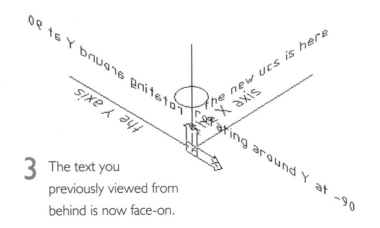

3 The text you previously viewed from behind is now face-on.

Editing Objects on a UCS

If you do not understand the orientation of your UCS, then editing commands (such as copy or offset) will not work the way you expect them to. This is easily illustrated using the viewport arrangement set up on the previous page.

Editing and drawing from behind a plane can be difficult, especially if you're inputting distance values such as in polar coordinates.

1 Copy the text 'the X axis'...

2 ...out to here.

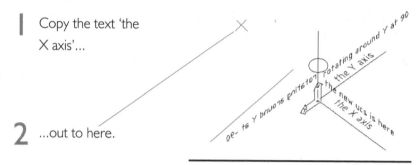

The drawing can be viewed from any position using the View command.

The copied text

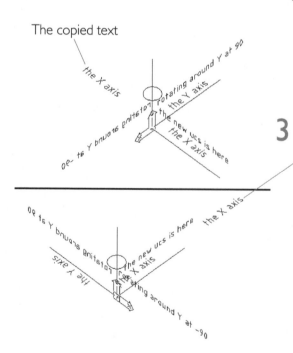

3 Notice the text's position in the lower viewport! Was it where you expected? Probably not, because you did not take into consideration the plane that the text was on originally.

Using 3 Points to Define a UCS

A UCS can be positioned by selecting three points on the drawing: one point sets the origin of the new UCS while the other two describe the orientation of the X and Y axes.

Start a new drawing and draw a rectangular shape anywhere on the screen. Make sure the sides of the shape are not parallel to the sides of the screen.

Issue the UCS command. Type N to select the option New and type 3 to select the 3 point option. AutoCAD will ask you to select a point for the new origin. Use the Object Snap mode INT (intersection) and pick the bottom left of the rectangular shape.

AutoCAD will now ask you to 'Specify point on the positive portion of the X axis'. Use the Object Snap to select the top right corner of the shape you drew.

Lastly AutoCAD will ask you to 'Specify point on the positive-Y portion of the UCS XY plane'. Use Object Snap to pick on the top left corner of the shape.

The UCS icon will orientate itself as you defined.

If the icon does not move into the position shown in the illustration use the OR option in the UCSICON command.

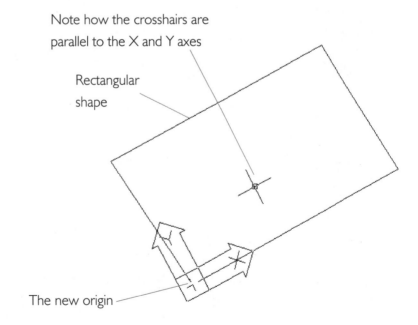

Note how the crosshairs are parallel to the X and Y axes

Rectangular shape

The new origin

The UCS Command Options

The UCS command controls the creation and movement of user coordinate systems. The UCS toolbar can be displayed by using the drop down menu View>Toolbars and placing an X in the UCS box. The options available are described here:

UCS: Issues the UCS command.

Named UCS: Opens the UCS Control dialogue box to rename or make a named UCS current.

UCS Previous: Returns you to the previous UCS used.

World UCS: Returns you to the World Coordinate System.

Object UCS: Allows you to set up a UCS by defining it as aligning to an object drawn on the screen.

Face UCS: Allows you to set up a UCS matching an existing UCS that you have already set up.

View UCS: Sets up a UCS parallel to the UCS current at the time you run the command.

Origin UCS: Allows you to set where the origin 0,0,0 is.

Z Axis vector UCS: Sets the direction for the Z axis.

3 Point UCS: Allows you to define a UCS by selecting three points on the drawing.

X Axis Rotate UCS: Sets the UCS by moving it around the X axis.

Y Axis Rotate UCS: Sets the UCS by moving it around the Y axis.

Z Axis Rotate UCS: Sets the UCS by moving it around the Z axis.

Apply UCS: Allows you to set existing viewports to the current viewport setting.

Wireframe Construction

The first step in the creation of a true 3D drawing is to produce a wireframe model. In this chapter you will create a wireframe and learn to construct it by using the UCS. The techniques for drawing from one plane or UCS to another are illustrated, as well as copying objects up the Z axis.

Covers

Chapter Thirteen

The Finished Wireframe Model

You can change from the 3D UCS icon to the 2D style using the Properties option under the UCSICON command. I recommend that you set the icon to the flat 2D style. It makes you aware of the plane you are working on.

The illustration below shows two views of a wireframe model. The following pages will show you how to construct this model and then place text on it.

You will start by creating the base and then adding the elements which are parallel to the base. Finally, the text is placed on each plane formed by the wireframe.

The exercise is an important one as it forms the basis for all true 3D modelling.

This shape, with the text, cannot be achieved using the pseudo 3D technique shown in chapter 6.

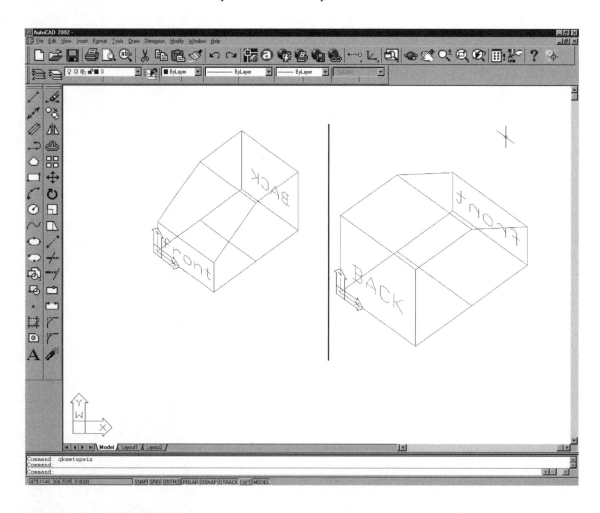

Laying the Base

Set up a standard A3 sheet to draw the shape. Use the viewports command to divide the screen vertically into two viewports. Name the viewport configuration 'plan14'.

Draw the following shape in the left viewport in the World Coordinate System:

When you save a vport arrangement, it is the arrangement of the vports you save, not their contents.

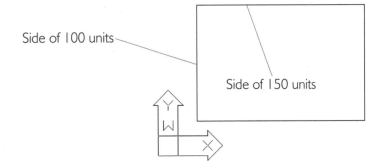

Side of 100 units

Side of 150 units

Now use the drop-down menu View>3D Views>Viewpoint Presets... Select to view the drawing in the left vport at 225 from the X axis and 45 from the XY plane. Click OK. You have just created a wireframe of the base of the shape. Draw a line from the midpoint of the 150 unit side to its opposite. Your screen will look similar to that below:

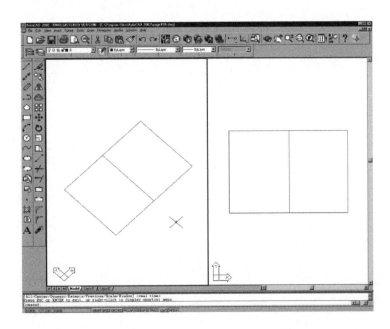

Constructing the Wireframe

Copy the 100 unit base line at the front up the Z axis 50 units, and then join up the copied line with the base. Here are the steps involved.

1 Issue the copy command. When asked to 'select objects', click on this line.

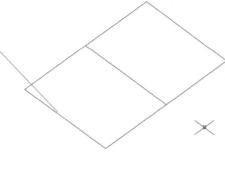

2 Press Enter. AutoCAD will ask 'Specify base point or displacement'. Type 0,0,0, and press Enter.

The wireframe is constructed so that later you may place 3D faces on it.

3 Lastly, AutoCAD will ask you to 'Specify second point of displacement'. Type in 0,0,50 and press Enter. This will copy the base line 50 units up the Z axis. The line CD is the result.

The line is copied up the Z axis 50 units.

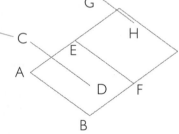

4 Carry out the same procedure to copy the line EF up the Z axis 100 units to become GH.

5 Issue the line command and draw a line from A to C to G, and then from B to D to H. Use the Object Snap 'end' for this.

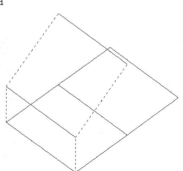

The drawing technique shown here allows you to copy objects from one plane to another using the x,y,z coordinates.

6 The right vport will not show any changes because it is a plan view of the drawing looking directly down the Z axis. Change the view in this vport to 45 degrees from the X axis and 45 degrees in the X–Y plane (see page 157). This will give a view of the object from behind.

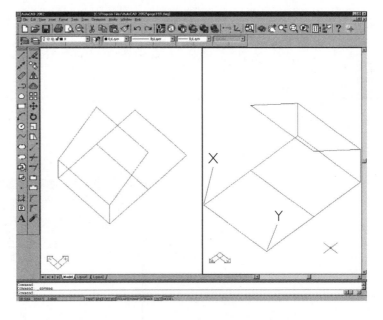

The Hide command will not hide any lines on a wireframe model.

7 Next, copy the line labelled XY 100 units up the Z axis to produce a line MN.

This completes the wireframe model. There was no need to define a new UCS in this case. You could draw from one plane to another, and use 3D coordinates to copy from one plane to another.

8 Join X to M to P. Join Y to N to Q.

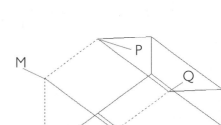

Using Layers

Layers should be used extensively in 3D drawings. The wireframe model just created should be placed on a separate layer before it becomes any more complex. Further layers can then be created to hold text or 3D faces (see the next chapter).

Create the following layers now:

1 A layer called TEXT. Assign to it the colour blue.

Make sure you are comfortable with the layers command before you work in 3D. See chapter 9.

2 A layer called WIREFRAME and assign to it the colour red.

3 Make the layer for TEXT current.

Text is set to blue

The wireframe layer is set current

The wireframe layer is set to red

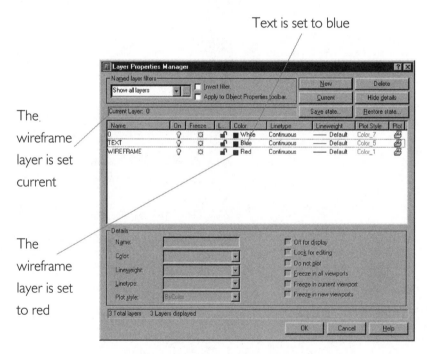

Now place the wireframe you have drawn onto the wireframe layer by using Modify>Properties drop-down menu. See page 107 'Moving Objects to Different Layers'.

Placing Text on a Plane

Once the layer TEXT is current you may then proceed to place text on the various planes of the wireframe model.

The text rotation angle of 0 is parallel to the X axis.

Text is easy to place if you move a UCS onto the plane you want the text on. To place text on the front plane, carry out the following steps:

A new UCS must be created for each plane you want to put the text on. Don't forget that you can give a UCS a name and return to it later by restoring it.

1. Move the UCS onto the front using the New 3 point option. If you set the running Object Snap mode to 'endpoint' you will find this easy.

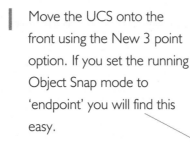

2. Clear all the Object Snap settings and issue the Text command. Select a point on the front face for the 'start point' of the text. The rotation angle will be 0 (zero) and the height of the text about 18 units.

3. Type in the text 'front' and press Enter twice to finish the command. The text will appear blue on the TEXT layer.

If the UCS icon does not follow you up to the new origin you must issue the UCSICON command and choose the option OR.

Using Vports as you Set Up a UCS

If you are still working with the vports arrangement set up on page 157, then you can move to the right vport and move the UCS to the back of the shape.

(page 157)

You can start most drawing/ editing commands in one viewport and end them in another.

If you find it too complex to move the UCS in the right viewport, then return to the left vport and do it there. The change will be reflected in the right vport.

The finished appearance is shown in the illustration below:

The view from the back shows the text inverted at the front

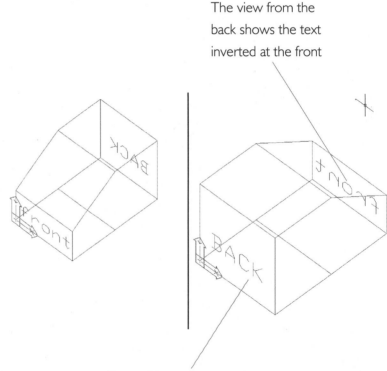

The UCS icon is placed flush against the back. The text will run parallel to the X axis by default

3D Faces

In this chapter you will place 3D faces on a wireframe model. 3D faces have edges. These edges may be visible or invisible. A visible 3D edge may show through in a rendered drawing at a point where you would prefer it to be invisible: consequently, it is important to be able to control edge visibility. This technique is also covered in this chapter.

Covers

Chapter Fourteen

What is a 3D Face?

The wireframe model created in the previous chapter is ready to take some 3D faces. A 3D face is a plane which is infinitely thin. Its value lies in the fact that it can hold a colour or a texture which may be found on a real object. You cannot see through a 3D face when the hide command is issued. You can see through a wireframe model.

Properties of 3D faces

All 3D faces are flat planes. Even curved surfaces in AutoCAD 2002 are made up of many small, flat planes. All 3D faces have edges. These edges are by default visible. They can be made invisible.

AutoCAD 2002 can place 3D faces on simple or complex shapes. A plane is placed between vertex points. The minimum number of vertices is three. There are several commands for producing 3D faces. Some of these are listed here:

3DFACE	Forms the simplest planar 3D face between 3 or 4 vertex points.
PFACE	Forms a simple 3D plane, but over an unlimited number of vertices.
TABSURF	Produces a planar or curved 3D face by projecting an object along an axis.
RULESURF	Produces a curved 3D face between two curved objects.
REVSURF	Creates a curved 3D face around a central axis.
EDGESURF	Produces a curved 3D face between four other objects.
3DMESH	Constructs a 3D face between any number of vertices.

Placing 3D Faces on the Wireframe

Open the drawing of the wireframe created in the previous chapter. Switch on the running Object Snap 'endpoint'.

Create a layer for each 3D face as follows:

- Layer TOP with the colour green

- Layer SLOPE with the colour red

- Layer FRONT with the colour blue

Set up layers to hold the 3D faces – this allows you to edit the faces

layer.

How the 3DFACE command works

Once the command is issued, AutoCAD will ask you to pick four points which define the planar area. The points (or vertices) must be picked in a clockwise or anticlockwise manner. Once the initial four points have been picked, AutoCAD will ask for further third and fourth points. This is useful if you want to add other 3D faces to the shape.

Try this now using the top of the wireframe shape:

A face takes on the colour of the layer it is placed on.

1 Make the layer TOP current.

2 Type 3DFACE (no spaces) at the command line and press Enter. AutoCAD will ask you for the first point of the face.

3 Pick the corners of the 'top' as AutoCAD asks you. Remember to pick in a circular manner.

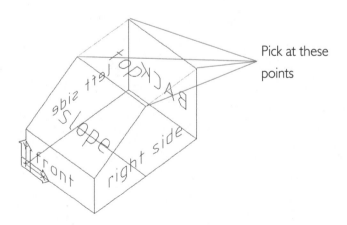

Pick at these points

4 To see if the 3D face appears, you must execute the SHADE command. You could also issue the HIDE command, but it will not hide the text.

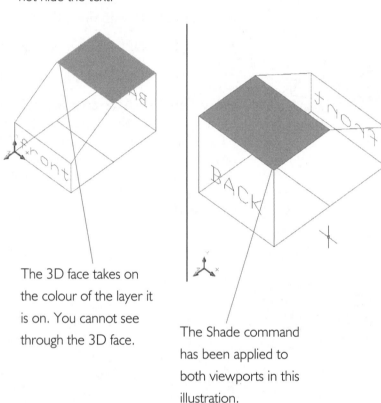

The 3D face takes on the colour of the layer it is on. You cannot see through the 3D face.

The Shade command has been applied to both viewports in this illustration.

5 You cannot proceed to place more faces while the shading is on the drawing. To continue, issue the Regen command and press Enter. Regen works only in the current viewport. To cause a regeneration in all the viewports, type 'regenall' and press Enter.

Visible 3D Face Edges

A face has an edge. The edge is visible by default, but can be made invisible either at the time the face is being placed in the drawing, or at a later stage.

To see the effect of the edges, try the following exercise.

Start a new drawing, using an A3 sheet with decimal units. Draw a four-sided shape similar to that in the illustration below. Next, set up a single layer called EDGES and assign the colour blue to it. Make it current:

A 3D face can be copied or moved by selecting the visible edge when you are asked to 'select objects'.

Apply a triangular 3D face by picking the vertices labelled 1, 2 and 3.

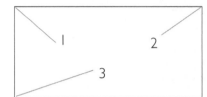

The 3D face has an edge on each side. The diagonal line is the edge of one side of the face.

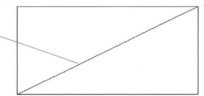

When the Shade command is applied, the overall face is visible.

Edges print and they are visible when a drawing is shaded or rendered. Edges can be made invisible.

Using Invisible Edges

Edges can be made invisible at the time you are applying a 3D face. To do this, insert the letter 'i' before you pick the point that begins the line that you want to be an invisible edge.

Again, draw a rectangular shape similar to that on the previous page. Place a similar three-sided 3D face on the shape in the following manner:

If you are covering an irregular shape with 3D faces, it is a good idea to use triangular shaped faces with invisible lines between them.

1 Issue the 3DFACE command at the command line.

2 Pick point 1 in the usual way when AutoCAD prompts 'first point'.

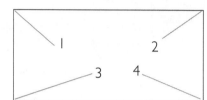

3 Now AutoCAD will prompt you for the 'second point'. Type the letter 'i' and press Enter. AutoCAD now knows that the next edge you draw will be invisible. Proceed to pick point 2.

4 Pick point 3 in the normal way (without the 'i') and press Enter to finish the command.

This edge is now invisible

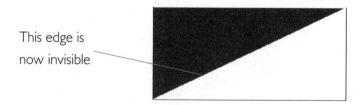

The 3D face will not have a visible edge between points 2 and 3.

Try placing another 3 sided 3D face between points 2, 3 and 4. Use a visible edge first and then an invisible edge. Shade the object each time to see the effect.

Drawing a Window

Placing a window on the side of a building requires the use of both visible and invisible edges using the 3DFACE command. The use of layers is also very important.

The window is defined by placing 3D faces on the walls – but not on the windows. Follow the steps here:

1 Construct the wireframe shown below with the outline of the window showing. Make sure the window outline is on its own layer.

2 Set up a separate layer for the 3D face that makes up the walls, and then make it current.

There are other ways the faces can be placed to form the window. You have control over the visibility of the edges.

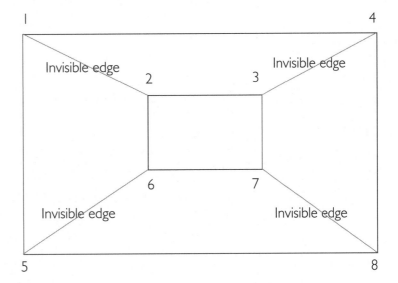

3 Place faces on the wireframe in the following sequence: 1,2,3,4; 5,6,7,8; 1,2,6,5; 4,3,7,8.

4 Shade the drawing. If you place the invisible edges in the wrong places, it will be self evident!

You might prefer to make the layers holding the window wireframe invisible before you shade the drawing. Try placing a door in a wall using the same technique.

Making Edges Visible/Invisible

Existing edges can be made visible or invisible using the system variable 'splframe,' or entering it as the command. In the window drawing on the previous page, you defined the wall itself with faces using invisible edges. The finished display looks as follows:

You must issue the Regen command after changing the Splframe system variable.

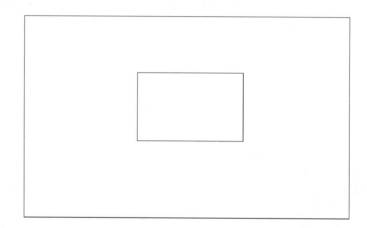

Now change the 'splframe' system variable by typing it at the command line and pressing Enter. AutoCAD will display 'Enter new value for SPLFRAME<0>'. Type in 1 and press Enter. You must now issue the 'regen' command to force AutoCAD to display all the 3D face edges.

The window drawing should look like the one below:

These edges were invisible until the 'splframe' variable was changed to 1

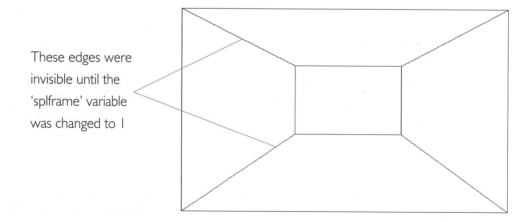

Rendering

Rendering is the application of textures and light to an object which has 3D faces. The 3D faces are visible, and so the texture applied to them is visible. The textures are stored in a basic library which AutoCAD 2002 holds. Textures simulate such materials as marble and wood.

Covers

Chapter Fifteen

Z-buffer Shaded Modelling

The procedure of rendering allows you to view the 3D faces on your model in various lighting conditions, and with various textures applied to the surfaces.

AutoCAD provides a toolbar to help you access the rendering options. The most basic rendering is called 'z-buffer' shaded modelling. To try this you must have first created a 3D wireframe model with some 3D faces on it.

I will use the wireframe created in Chapters 13–14 to illustrate some of the issues in rendering.

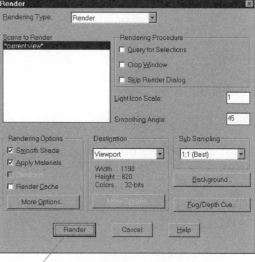

If you want to hide the UCS icon, issue the UCSICON command and select the option 'off'.

Open the wireframe model with the 3D faces. If you have several viewports configured, set the view for a single viewport.

Now issue the render command: View>Render>Render. The dialogue box above appears. Make sure your settings are the same and then click on Render.

At this point, the rendered image will not be too dissimilar to a shaded one. The light shining on the object is the default camera setting, which is where your eye is now. These settings can all be changed.

Letting the Sun Shine

AutoCAD allows you to control the light that shines on the drawing. To set the light source as the sun, try the following:

1 Issue the command View>Render>Light.

2 Click on the New drop-down arrow, and select Distant Light.

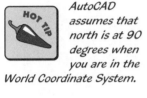

AutoCAD assumes that north is at 90 degrees when you are in the World Coordinate System.

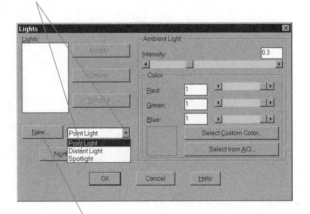

3 Click the New button. The follow dialogue appears. Type SUN in here.

4 To select the position of the sun, use the Sun Angle Calculator. To do this click on this button.

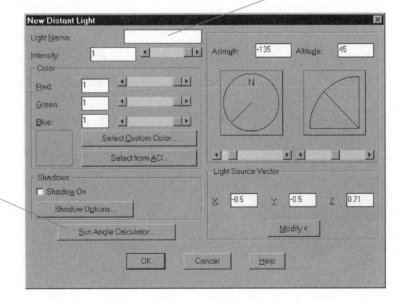

5 Instead of trying to calculate the position of the sun yourself you can let AutoCAD do it for you by telling it where you are positioned on Earth. Click on Geographic Location.

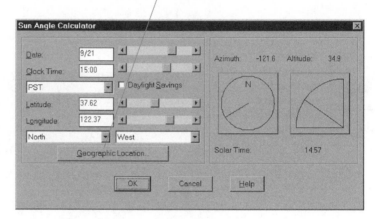

Try different light settings to get a feel for how AutoCAD 2002 is lighting the image.

6 Set the geographical location as it is in this dialogue box. If you set up a different one, you will not get the same rendering.

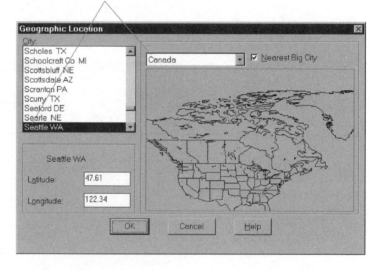

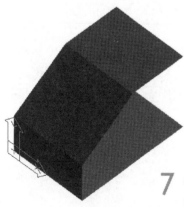

7 Click OK in all the open dialogues boxes to return to the Drawing Editor. Then issue the Render command to see the results.

Selecting Textures for 3D Faces

AutoCAD contains a library of textures you can apply to the surface of an object. To look in the texture library and select one, follow the steps below:

1   Select View>Render>Materials Library... The Materials Library dialogue is displayed.

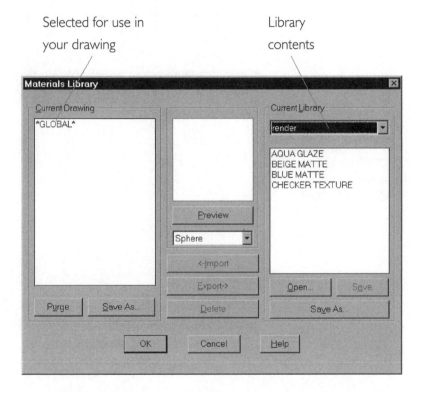

Selected for use in your drawing

Library contents

2   In the Current Library list, select CHECKER TEXTURE. Click on Preview to see what it is like.

3   Click on Import to add it to the selected list on the left. All textures on the left can be used in the drawing.

4   Click on OK.

To assign a material to a 3D face, see the next page.

Assigning Materials to an Object

1 Display the Materials dialogue box by selecting View>Render>Materials.

2 Select CHECKER TEXTURE in the left column.

3 We will attach the text to a layer in the wireframe model. To do this, click on the 'By Layer' button. The Attach by Layer dialogue box is displayed.

Always develop a 3D drawing using layers. The importance of layers can be appreciated in this application of textures.

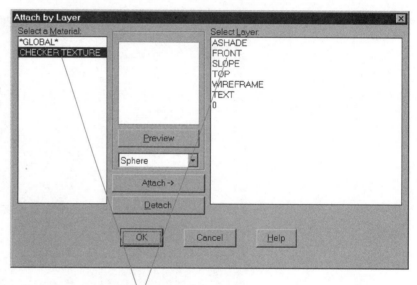

4 Highlight the texture in the left column and then highlight the layer Front in the right column, and finally click on Attach.

5 Click OK where required to return to the drawing. Select Render. The layer Front will render with the texture you assigned to it.

Working with Paperspace

In this chapter you will look in some detail at how AutoCAD 2002 uses the Paperspace Layouts. Paperspace is used to help in the presentation of drawings. It is particularly valuable for presenting the same drawing at different scales on the same page. Once mastered, it becomes an indispensable tool.

Covers

Chapter Sixteen

Why Use Paperspace?

Using layers is important because they can help filter out objects in the drawing by freezing selected viewports.

Traditionally AutoCAD drawings have been produced in Model Space at real world size (1=1). It is possible to plot a drawing directly from Model Space once you have worked out the plot scale. The major restriction on using Model Space to output the drawing is that you can only plot at one scale. By using Paperspace it is possible to plot two or three views of the same drawing at different scales on a single sheet of paper.

Paperspace is accessed through the tabs at the bottom of the Drawing Editor named Layout 1 and Layout 2. The word 'layout' refers to the layout of the drawing on the sheet of paper selected for printing/plotting.

Before you carry out the procedures in this chapter, create a simple drawing as follows:

The tiled viewports created in Model Space cannot be plotted.

Use the Quick Wizard to set up an electronic sheet of paper 42000 by 29700 mm. This is 100 times larger than a standard A3 sheet (420 by 297). Now execute a Zoom – All and set the Grid to 1000. Create two layers called TEXT and DRAINAGE. This will be used to illustrate some Paperspace settings. Create a simple drawing similar to the illustration below. Place the text on the TEXT layer and the dashed lines on the DRAINAGE layer. The rest of the drawing should be on layer 0.

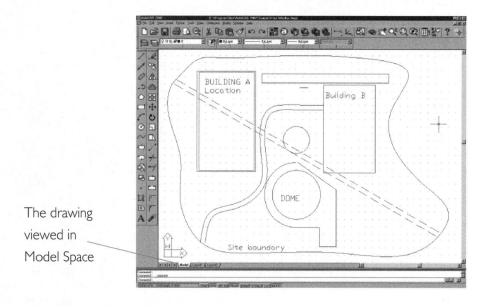

The drawing viewed in Model Space

Using the Default Layout 1

Before Paperspace may be used you must decide on the following:

1.   The printer/plotter you wish to use.

2.   The size of the paper you wish to plot on.

Now carry out the procedure below to plot the drawing on an A3 page at a scale of 1:100.

| Make sure the drawing you set up on page 178 is open in Model Space and then click on the Layout 1 tab. The following screen is displayed. Select your printer.

If the settings you make here are later found to be incorrect you can change them by right-clicking on the Layout tab and selecting Page Setup.

Make sure the Plot Device tab is current.

Select your print device by clicking on the down-arrow.

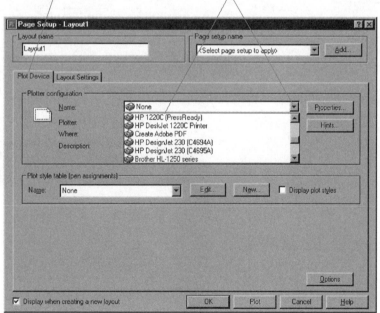

2   The plotter/printer you select determines the range of sheet sizes that are available. Now click on the Layout Settings tab in the dialogue box.

3 Select an A3 page. Make sure that Layout is selected under 'Plot area' and that the plot scale is 1:1.

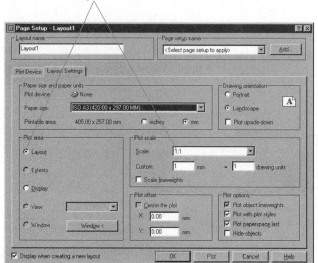

4 These settings will now be used by AutoCAD to set up a simple layout of one viewport. A scale will still need to be set. Click on OK to continue.

The paper border (A3)

The border of the viewport

The Paperspace icon

The selected Layout tab

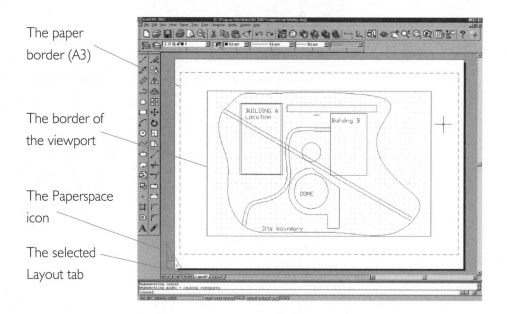

The Default Layout Page's Anatomy

The following should be noted about the layout (see page 180).

1. The dashed line around the drawing represents the page size that you selected in step 3.

2. The continuous line inside that is the border of a single default viewport that AutoCAD has offered. This can be changed later.

3. The display is in Paperspace. This is indicated in the following ways:

    (a) The UCS icon has been replaced by the Paperspace icon.

    (b) The word 'MODEL' on the Status Bar has been replaced by 'PAPER'

    (c) When the cursor is moved around the screen it passes over both the drawing and the paper border. You are unable to edit the drawing.

4. This is a preview of how the drawing will appear when it is plotted at 1:1 on an A3 page.

You can return to the Paperspace view by a single click on 'MODEL' on the Status Bar.

Status Bar   Click on PAPER to access the drawing

Model Space within Paperspace

You can return to Model Space within this viewport by a single click on the word 'PAPER' on the Status Bar. Try this now and note the following:

1. The UCS icon appears in the viewport and a heavy border surrounds it indicating that it is current.

2. You can edit the drawing and use the normal drawing/editing commands.

3. You are unable to move the cursor outside the viewport.

Scaling the Drawing – Method 1

When a default Layout is displayed for the first time, the complete drawing is always displayed to fit in the viewport regardless of the size of the viewport. You will need to set the scale for the drawing before it is plotted.

Setting the scale while in Paperspace.

1 Make sure that 'PAPER' is selected on the Status Bar.

2 Click on the border of the viewport. It should highlight with grips if you are successful.

3 Right-click and select Properties from the floating menu. The Properties box is displayed listing the properties of the viewport.

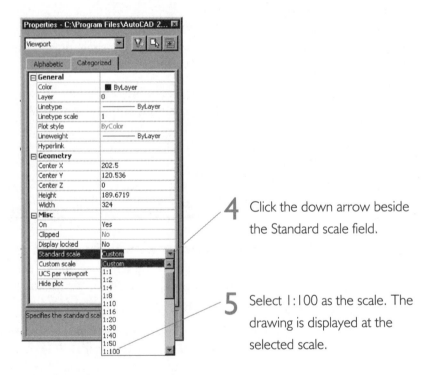

4 Click the down arrow beside the Standard scale field.

5 Select 1:100 as the scale. The drawing is displayed at the selected scale.

If the viewport does not show the region of the drawing you want displayed, use the Pan command to reposition it as Pan does not affect the scale. To use Pan make sure 'MODEL' is displayed on the Status Bar.

Scaling the Drawing – Method 2

The drawing can be scaled while in Model view when in Paperspace using the Zoom command.

Setting the scale while in Paperspace Model view

Zoom in on the area of the drawing that interests you before you apply the XP option. This will ensure you do not have to Pan too much to find the objects you want to see.

1 Make sure that the Layout tab has been selected and ensure that 'MODEL' is selected on the Status Bar.

2 The viewport will now display the UCS icon. The viewport will also display the heavy border indicating that it is current.

3 Issue the Zoom command.

4 One of the options is XP which means 'times paper'. To set the drawing at 1:100 enter '1/100xp' and press Enter (or the Spacebar).

5 The drawing will display at 1:100. If it does not display the area you are interested in, then use the Pan command to position it.

Plotting the scaled drawing

Drawings using the Paperspace layouts should be plotted at 1:1. In this example an A3 layout is being plotted to an A3 page at 1:1. The scaling of the drawing has already been carried out on the sheet itself.

Be aware of the difference between the Model tab and MODE/PAPER button on the Status Bar.

Before the Plot command is issued make sure that you have the word 'PAPER' displayed on the Status Bar. Once the command is issued select the Plot Settings tab and set the Scale at 1:1. You may, of course, select other scales.

Use the Full Preview to see the results of your settings. If the settings are accurate you will hardly notice that you have entered the Preview mode as the Layouts are themselves previews of the drawing.

Status Bar

PAPER must be here before you plot the Layout

SNAP GRID ORTHO POLAR OSNAP OTRACK LWT PAPER

Working with Paperspace Viewports

The Layout 1 and Layout 2 tabs offer just a single viewport in Paperspace mode. It is possible to edit the viewport border as though it were a normal drawing object. In fact it is a drawing object that 'clips' a view through the paper down to the drawing. Here are some edits you may like to consider.

Resizing the viewport

1 The Status Bar must display the word 'PAPER'.

2 Click on the border of the viewport to display the grips.

Resizing the viewport does not affect the scale that has been applied to the drawing.

3 Activate a grip by clicking on it (it will turn red) and using the Stretch command (offered on the Command line) move the grip. The viewport is resized as you do so.

4 Note how the drawing stays in the same position on the screen; this can be used to hide parts of the drawing.

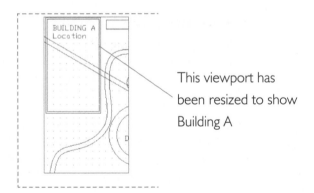

This viewport has been resized to show Building A

Moving the viewport

1 Activate a grip by clicking on it (it will turn red) and using the Move command (offered on the Command line when you press the Spacebar).

2 Note how the drawing moves with the viewport.

Deleting and Creating Viewports

Viewports may be deleted. Their removal does not affect the original Model Space drawing.

Deleting a viewport

Once the viewports are created they may be moved around so that they are overlapping.

1 The Status Bar must display the word 'PAPER'.

2 Click on the border of the viewport to display the grips.

3 Click the Erase command or press the Delete key on the keyboard.

4 Note how the drawing disappears also. The drawing, however, is not deleted. You can check that it still exists by clicking on the Model tab at the bottom of the Drawing Editor.

If there is space on the Layout you have created you may create new viewports. Viewports can be any shape you decide on. Viewports may also be deleted.

Creating a viewport

1 The Status Bar must display the word 'PAPER'. It will return you to the last Layout you worked on.

2 Type the command Mview (or the alias 'mv'). AutoCAD will offer several options. Just click two points on the screen to define a window the size of the viewport you want.

Viewport borders should be assigned to a separate layer rather than all other objects in the drawing. This will allow you to control their visibility.

3 The drawing will appear in the viewport just defined.

4 To make a circular vport simply draw a circle on a blank area of the sheet and issue the Mview command; select the option Object and click on the circle. The circle becomes a viewport.

More about Paperspace Viewports

The following layout is composed of four viewports and some text. The text was entered on to the A3 page at real-world size (in this example it is 4 mm high). I will now make some changes to the layout to make it look more professional. Remember that how it appears here is how it will look on paper.

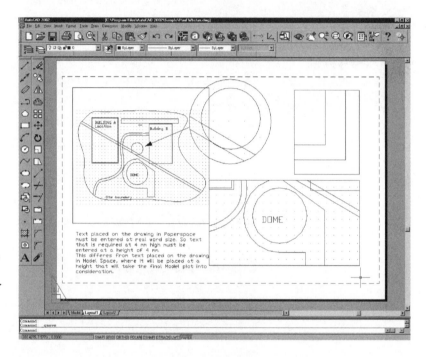

Viewport borders can be created using linetypes other than the default continuous type.

Removing the borders from the viewports

A good way to do this is to create a separate layer for the borders and hide or freeze it. In this case I made a layer called MVIEW BORDERS and carried out the following steps:

1. The Status Bar must display the word 'PAPER'.

2. Click on the border of each of the viewports to display the grips and drop the borders onto the layer MVIEW BORDERS by selecting it from the Object Properties toolbar.

3. Now hide the viewport by clicking on the lightbulb icon to switch the layer off. The borders will disappear.

Scaling the linetypes in the viewports

Linetypes, such as the dashed linetype used in this drawing can appear magnified up or down when the scaling is applied to the viewports. The system variable PSLTSCALE allows AutoCAD to calculate how the linetype should be displayed at different viewport scales.

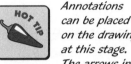

Annotations can be placed on the drawing at this stage. The arrows in the illustration were drawn with the Pline command in Paperspace. They will not appear in Model view.

1 The Status Bar must display the word 'PAPER'.

2 Type PSLTSCALE at the command line and enter a value of 1 (the default) and press Enter.

3 Use the View drop down menu to Regen All.

Note the linetype scaling and the absence of the viewport boundaries

A layout can be named by right-clicking on it and selecting Rename from the floating menu. Enter a description name such as 'A3–4 VIEWS'.

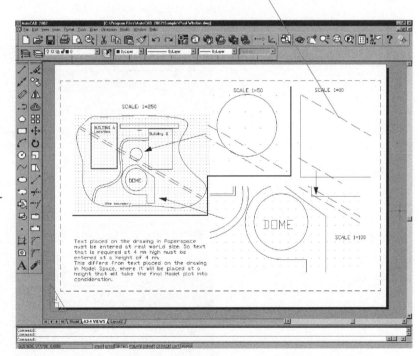

Freezing Individual Viewports

At times it will be necessary to hide some objects in a selected viewport, while allowing them to be visible in another. This is carried out by freezing individual layers in the different viewports. For example, to hide the drainage dashed linetype in one viewport and leave it displayed in all the others, carry out the following steps:

1 The Status Bar must display the word 'MODEL' while in a Layout.

2 Make a viewport current by clicking in it. Make sure it is the one that holds the linetype that you want to hide.

3 Now select the Layers icon on the Object Properties toolbar.

4 Click on 'Show Details' if necessary.

5 Click on the DRAINAGE layer.

6 In the Details part of the dialogue box place a tick in 'Freeze in current viewport' and select OK. The DRAINAGE line will be invisible in the selected viewport.

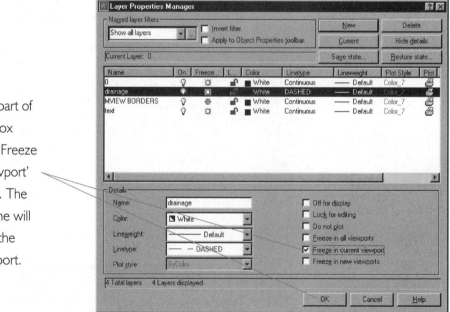

Index

E

F

G

H

I

L